Conversation

Sidhe

David Spangler

Other Works by
David Spangler

Dedication

This book is dedicated to Mariel and her companions without whom this book would not be possible.

It is dedicated to my partner, Jeremy Berg whose beautiful paintings made the Sidhe Card Deck possible and whose support has made all my work much easier than it would be otherwise.

It is dedicated to John Matthews, R.J. Stewart, and Orion Foxwood, who pioneered a way for me to follow.

It is dedicated to all who participated in my online classes, forums, and gatherings to explore with me the mystery and wonder of the Sidhe and their role in our lives.

It is dedicated to all my Lorian colleagues who make this work an ongoing delight and an honor.

It is dedicated to my wife, Julia, for whom no words are ever sufficient but who fills my life with Joy and Light.

And it is dedicated to the Sidhe and to Humanity as together we discover ways to heal, honor, and bless Gaia and all the life that shares this world with us on all its levels of being.

Conversations with the Sidhe

Card Illustrations and Cover Art by Jeremy Berg

Published by Lorian Press
686 Island View Drive
Camano Island, WA 98282

ISBN: 978-0-936878-67-6

Spangler/David
Conversations with the Sidhe/David Spangler

First Edition June 2014

Printed in the United States of America

0 9 8 7 6 5 4 3 2 1

www.lorian.org

Contents

INTRODUCTION
The Beginning

Every fairy tale has a beginning. For this one, it's in 2004, when my friend and Lorian colleague Jeremy Berg, the owner and publisher of Lorian Press, published *The Sidhe*, a book by the British spiritual teacher and author John Matthews. *Sidhe* (pronounced *shee*) is, according to John, the "oldest known name for the faery races of Ireland" and means the "people of peace." In the book, John describes his contact with one of the Sidhe and tells of the various conversations and messages that ensued.

This book became very popular and eventually led to a demand for more material about the Sidhe. In fact, a friend of ours, Adrienne McDunn, who had her own history of contact with the Sidhe, received a message from them that they would like to see a card deck produced that would be a point of contact between their world and ours. She approached Jeremy who in turn contacted John Matthews. Interestingly, he discovered that John, not knowing anything of the message Adrienne had received, had himself independently received a similar request from his Sidhe contact.

Unfortunately, although he certainly had the knowledge and skills to do so and would have liked to undertake such a project, John was too busy with other projects at the time to do so. Knowing my love of designing card decks (I had already designed two for Lorian Press, the *Manifestation Card Deck* and *The Soul's Oracle*), Jeremy then asked if I'd like to create a card deck about the Sidhe. I was intrigued, but unlike John or R.J. Stewart or Orion Foxwood, two other friends and authors who have written several books about the Faery realms, I knew very little about these beings. While I have had extensive contact for nearly seventy years with the invisible, subtle worlds of spirit and those who dwell upon them, I had had virtually no communication with the Sidhe or indeed with any Faery being that I knew of. So I told Jeremy that I didn't feel I was capable of such a task. It seemed that the Sidhe's request would go unfulfilled.

In the winter of 2011, however, something unexpected happened that changed everything. Taking a break from writing, I was sitting on the sofa in my living room and just staring out the window at the trees and bushes beyond when I felt a presence in the room behind me. Turning around, I saw in my mind's eye a swirling, shifting, radiant mist in the air near the fire place. At the same time I felt another mind in touch with my own and heard it say, "I am one of the Sidhe, and I've come to help you with the card deck." This being no sooner said this than there flashed into my mind a complete picture of what a Sidhe card deck would look like when laid out and the major components of what such a deck should contain. There were few details—they came later—but the basic pattern was very clear.

The initial contact was very brief, lasting no more than five minutes, but it was long enough and comprehensive enough that I knew beyond any doubt that I could create a Sidhe-oriented card deck. With this new-found confidence, I phoned Jeremy, explained what had happened and asked if he was still interested in publishing a Sidhe deck. He certainly was, and so the project began.

In the previous card decks I had done, Jeremy's daughter Deva had been the artist, and she had been truly inspired. But she had become a new mother and was unable to undertake another project. So Jeremy, who had done no painting at all up to this point, decided he would try to paint all the cards. As it turned out, just as the Sidhe inspired me with the overall structure and use of the cards, they inspired Jeremy with the images for the cards, who proceeded to produce a beautiful and powerful set of images.

In the process, a remarkable three-way partnership unfolded between Jeremy and me and the Sidhe. The ones who came to me were a woman and two male associates or companions. For the most part, she was the spokesperson, the one guiding the project, but occasionally, one or another of the two men would communicate with me.

The nature of this contact was different from anything I had experienced before and initially was difficult to maintain. But over time, it became easier as both the Sidhe and I adjusted to each other's energy characteristics. However, it was evident to me that whatever the Sidhe might be, they were not subtle beings or beings of spirit such as I was accustomed to perceiving. There was a strong sense of physicality about them, even though it was obviously a different wavelength or frequency of physicality than that of my body. Initially, they seemed to me wispy and diaphanous, hard for me to focus upon and hold, like trying to grasp quicksilver. I would sense movement, like white banners or ribbons wrapping around me and then fading away, but surrounding me with a definite sense of presence. They interacted with my own energy in a way I had not previously known, and it required me to adjust my own methods of attunement and perception to this new experience. But as we worked together, it became easier to maintain the contact. It even came to the point where I could perceive their forms, something I had not been able to do at the beginning of our engagement together. Interestingly, this difficulty of contact and the fact that I had to work for it was one factor that convinced me it was genuine.

For this project, the Sidhe had guidelines. For instance, we were asked not to portray the Sidhe themselves in the cards. They wished to prevent imposing a particular form either upon the Sidhe themselves or upon the imagination of a person using the cards. A second reason was that they are attempting to move past the older images that we've created of what they look like. This was confirmed for me later in a conversation with John Matthews when he said the Sidhe had told him to stop thinking of them as if they were knights and ladies of some medieval faerie kingdom. "We are of the present and the future," he was told, and I have received similar messages as well.

Another request was that there could be no more than thirty-three cards in the deck. I have no idea why that particular number was a limit, but both Jeremy and I received this information independently of each other. Obviously this deck was not to be anything like a traditional Tarot which has seventy-eight cards.

From the standpoint of the Sidhe who contacted me, the overall purpose of the card deck was to act as a point of potential contact between a user and the energetic realm of the Sidhe. This contact would take place within the imagination and the subtle energy fields of the user and would be unique to each person. And in the years since the deck was published, this is exactly how it has worked out for the many people now using it.

After the card deck was published in the late Fall of 2011, I thought that might be the end of it. Months went by without any contact or with very little, in part due to medical issues I was having which required one surgery after another. But then in the late spring and early summer of 2012 the woman returned, her presence stronger and clearer than before. Communication was much easier than it had been at any time in our work on the card deck. Apparently progress had been made in our connection.

They were following up on the work we'd done the year before in creating the card deck. These cards were part of a larger project to enable greater engagement and collaboration between human beings and the Sidhe, and now she wanted to begin exploring more deeply just what this might mean.

Communication with subtle beings is generally nothing like communication between people, at least in my experience, and the same is true with communications with the Sidhe. There is a verbal, telepathic element to it, but mostly I am drawn into field of impressions, meanings, images, feelings, and thoughts which I then need to put into words.

In this process, I have her help to ensure I get the content and meaning correct, and at times she may suggest or even insist on particular wording. It really is like translating from another language. As much as possible, I have tried to capture the feel of her. She was serious, but at the same time there was lightness and a sense of joy and humor that was present as well. I have felt this every time I've been in contact with the Sidhe. They seem to me a fundamentally joyous people.

Along with the joy, I have also felt a deep wisdom within this woman. It's not always a human wisdom; it's a wisdom of stars and forests, landscapes and living creatures, a wisdom of the connections between all things. But at no time did she present herself as an all-knowing teacher or in any way as my superior. She came as a colleague and a friend, bearing her gifts but open to receiving from me—and from other humans—as well.

I called her *Mariel*. Her actual name is impossible for me to translate; the Sidhe language as I experience it is melodious and reminiscent to me of natural sounds, like a brook murmuring as if flows over stones. Much of their language seems to me one of energy exchange as much as of an exchange of thoughts or sounds. But "Mariel" seemed to evoke the quality and feel of her presence for me, and she seemed to like it as well, so we settled on it as the name I would use.

It seemed to me that she was some kind of a priestess. In one conversation between us, she clarified this image.

I am not a "priestess," at least not in the way that you think. Oh, there may be similarities in that I work with various subtle energies, but I am more artist than priestess. I am like a weaver, skilled in touching and blending together threads of energy and life drawn from a variety of dimensions of reality. I suppose you could think of me as akin to those you call shamans in your world.

4

One of the other two Sidhe seemed to step forward then—at least his energy took precedence in my consciousness—and said, "She is one who tends the flow of life. Where she is and where she goes, life flows more fully." And as he spoke, I had an interesting image of her laying her hand on a boulder and water gushing forth from the solid rock. She seemed to find this image both exaggerated and amusing, but even if not fully accurate, it conveyed his high regard and respect for her. What truly came across to me was a feeling of the deep friendship between these three individuals. I had the sense of a relationship that had lasted and matured over a very long period of time.

Over the years, as the Sidhe and I have become more familiar with each other, their appearance has changed, moving from a wispy, cloud-like form to that of individuals looking altogether human, though with a signature grace and beauty. As Mariel herself describes later in our conversations, some of this change is deliberate in order to make easier contact with human beings. On the other hand, too much can be made of their appearance, which is one reason they expressly forbade Jeremy or I making any images of them in the card deck. One of the challenges we have as human beings is that we pay overly much attention to externals, to the forms and surfaces of things. In the process, we deaden our capacity to perceive more deeply into the realm of meaning and being. We become caught up with what something *looks* like and overlook what it *feels* like.

I am accustomed to many years of working with subtle beings that have no particular appearance but who are rich in meaning and presence; not having a specific exterior to capture the mind and eye, the *interior* is freer to express and to be known. This is true for the Sidhe as well. Yes, it's true that I now have a much easier time communicating with Mariel than I did when she first appeared, but this has nothing to do with whether she has a form I can recognize or not. It has much to do with simply learning to get on the same wavelength together, and yes, appearance can play a role in this. But the Mariel with whom I communicate today is in every important way that counts the same as the Mariel who first appeared in my living room in the winter of 2011 to describe the structure of a deck of cards. The same spirit, the same presence, the same meaningfulness is there. I'll talk about this more later in the context of the most recent communications.

My conversations with Mariel have continued on and off, though with increasing regularity, over the past two years. Part I of this book recounts these initial communications. When I began this book, I thought I would simply arrange these messages chronologically to show the progression as our contact developed. However, the topics and themes jump around, partly based on questions that I or others had and partly based on Mariel's intents. Also, I might start a conversation on a particular subject and then lose the contact for one reason or another. Days or even weeks might go by, then Mariel would come again and pick up the conversation as if no break had occurred. At such times, she might go back and amplify or even correct some of the notes and transcriptions I had made earlier.

For this reason, I ended up deciding that I would organize the conversations by topic instead of by chronology. Since many of the comments were timeless, I felt that it didn't matter so much which came first and which came later. In this way, I feel I've preserved the clarity and intent of the messages and made them easier to follow.

These days I do all my teaching online. Through the Lorian Association, I offer a number of classes in Incarnational Spirituality and in partnering with the subtle worlds. After several months of developing conversations with Mariel, in January of 2014, she came and asked if Jeremy and I would sponsor an experimental online class that she would teach with us. We both said yes, of course, but neither of us had any idea what to expect.

The class was held for six weeks in April and May of 2014, and we needn't have worried. Mariel and her colleagues came through with a strength and clarity that I had not experienced with them before, creating a field of energy that resulted in more communications from her than in the whole of the year preceding. All of these conversations make up Part II of this book.

During the class, Mariel suggested a number of exercises that we could do to enhance a connection with her realm through attuning to what she called "star-energies". Part III contains all of these. I conclude with thoughts on working with the Sidhe and how to incorporate their presence and gifts into our lives; in other words, how to "bring it home".

I want to emphasize that all these conversations are my best translation of what Mariel has had to say. They should really be taken as "field notes", not as "holy writ." I write and publish an esoteric journal, *Views from the Borderland*, four times a year. In it I share my ongoing research and experiences in engaging with the subtle worlds. But I've also discussed my contacts with Mariel and the Sidhe. Indeed, some of the conversations and exercises in this book were first presented to the subscribers of this journal. At the beginning of each issue is the following statement:

> *All the material contained in this journal is based on my personal observations and experiences. While I present it as accurately and clearly as I am able, it is subject to the limitations of my own background, understanding, bias, perceptual abilities, and skills of interpretation. While I have years of experience in this area, I am most certainly not infallible. I am still exploring and learning. This being said, I invite you to join with me in this exploration. If anything you read here resonates with your mind and heart, may it be a blessing and a help to you.*

The same sentiment applies here. I view this book as part of an exploration and experiment, one that is still evolving. As a result, I regard all information here as provisional. It is as accurate as I can make it given my skills at the moment and the nature of the contact, and I stand by all that is contained in this book. But nothing is ever final. As both my skills and the contacts improve, deeper insights and newer information may cast new light upon material that has already been recorded.

As Mariel emphasizes over and over again, her mission and that of the Sidhe whom she represents is not to focus attention upon them but to help us know ourselves in new and empowering ways. As human beings, we hold keys to the future well-being of the Earth and all upon it. The Sidhe very much want us to find these keys within us and learn how to use them for the benefit of all. This will not change. This is a true and accurate vision.

It's to this vision that this book is dedicated.

PART I

INITIAL CONVERSATIONS

CHAPTER ONE
Cousins

After the Card Deck of the Sidhe was published in 2011, contact with Mariel or with other Sidhe dropped off, with one exception. A five minute drive from our house is a neighborhood park which contains what I think of as a "pocket forest." Surrounded by suburban houses, this patch of woods is nevertheless dense enough that when I'm in it, I can feel like I'm out in the wilderness. No buildings of any kind are visible from its depths.

Over the years of hiking in this park, which also contains wetlands and a large meadow, I've come to know the nature spirit that overlights the forest. It has a curious energy about it that comes from having adapted to the human communities that are all around it, and I often have the sense when I visit this place that it's studying us in an interested and loving way.

One sunny afternoon I drove to the park to spend some time walking in the forest. I parked in the parking lot of the park and walked towards the forest. As I came to its edge and stepped onto the path that led into it, I was surprised to clairvoyantly see a tall, stately male figure appear and stand next to me. I realized that it was one of the Sidhe. Apparently, the work I had been doing with Mariel and her colleagues in creating the card deck had sensitized me to the Sidhe energies.

This being walked with me for most of the time I was in the forest. We didn't say much, but I delighted in being in his presence and he seemed to enjoy my own. He said that he often came to this forest as he knew the overlighting spirit which was also present in his realm. Of course, most humans never knew he was present. But he recognized the influence of Sidhe energies around me, so he decided to make contact.

Whereas I had seen Mariel as a formless swirl of Light most of the time, I saw this individual very clearly, no doubt due to his greater familiarity and association with the etheric and physical realms. He was well over six feet in height, was dressed all in white, and had something on his head which at times seemed like antlers and at times seemed like feathers or a headdress of some nature. He exuded great strength and a sense of kindliness and also curiosity.

I have been an asthmatic all my life, and often when I'm out walking in nature, I can get short of breath. One part of the trail through this forest is very steep, and invariably I get to huffing and puffing as I climb up it. He noticed this and asked if he could help. I said yes, and to my surprise, he stepped into my body so that I could feel his Light within me and around me, and when he did so, I felt strength and breath surging through me. The difficulty with breathing left entirely, and I charged up this hill with no problem. It was an amazing experience.

When I reached the end of the forest path and started back towards the parking lot, this being said farewell and faded away.

The next time I visited the park, this Sidhe individual came out of the forest half-way towards the parking lot to meet me, and we walked back into the forest together. It seemed that this side-effect of working on the Sidhe deck was going to continue, and I looked forward to getting to know this individual better. However, life intervened. A blockage of scar tissue had developed in my urinary tract as a result of several years of surgeries to remove recurring tumors in my bladder. To deal with the situation, 2012 became a year of one surgery after another. In order to protect my kidney from swelling, a nephrostomy tube was temporarily inserted in my back to allow the kidney to drain. I called it my "outdoor plumbing." Interestingly, I was aware that there was a small but constant leak of subtle energy from out of my back as a result of this tube.

During this time, I went to the park for a walk. As before, I found my Sidhe friend coming out of the forest to greet me, and then he stopped. I became aware that he was suddenly aware of the nephrostomy tube, which I wore hidden under my clothes, and most likely of more besides, for he said, "I can't approach you. You're body is compromised at the moment, and I don't know how it will react to my energy. It is safer if I do not intrude." Then he disappeared.

Working with subtle forces is a form of physical effort that does take energy. Apart from the Sidhe in the forest, I realized that most of my subtle colleagues were keeping their distance as well to give my body a chance to cope with what was happening to it and to heal without also having to deal with their energies. During this time, I received one short message from Mariel that basically said "Get well. We'll talk when this is over." For the time being at least, my engagement with the Sidhe seemed to be over.

Therefore it came as a surprise to me when in July, Mariel made a brief appearance, I think to check up on me. Fortunately, it was during a three-month hiatus between surgeries, so my energy was "up" and I was feeling pretty good. Unfortunately, it was right after the massacre in Aurora, Colorado, when, on the night of July 20, 2012, during a midnight showing of the movie *The Dark Knight Rises*, a madman opened fire on a theater filled with people, killing twelve and wounding seventy. I was feeling sorrow about this event and, as I worked in the kitchen, I was also thinking about the ripples of negative energies that this event had caused in the subtle environments closest to the physical plane.

I suddenly became aware that an invisible presence had just appeared standing next to me, and as I turned on my inner perceptions to see who or what it was, I was surprised to discover it was Mariel.

It was a tentative contact. I felt that she came with a purpose, which included seeing how I was doing but went beyond that. However, sensing my mood and thoughts, she apparently set that purpose aside and directed her comments to the sorrow I was feeling. Her thoughts also reflected her own experience in dealing with negative energies within the earth's subtle environment. As she spoke, I could feel her compassion but also her own vulnerability while entering the energy fields close to the earth in order to communicate with me.

It was a short contact, and immediately after she withdrew, I wrote down what she had to say. Here are her comments:

We sympathize with your sorrow. We also are not immune to the shocks that run through the energy fields of humanity and of the earth itself. The sufferings and pains of your world reverberate into our own. More precisely, they reverberate throughout the planet as a whole, and our realm is a part of this world just as yours is. So we cannot be unaffected.

This is particularly true for those of us who have chosen to live and work close to the physical plane in order to bridge the gaps between us. Think of us as flimsy, wispy clouds when we draw close to your world. The winds of your emotions can blow into and through us unless we are anchored by your calmness and love.

Of course we stand in our own strength as well, and my partner here [a male Sidhe whom I can sense in the background as she speaks] laughs at the image of me as a wispy cloud, but there is still a truth to this. We have ways of protecting ourselves and minimizing or even canceling out the impact in some instances, but those of us who are working at the boundary to make future collaborative partnerships possible surrender some of these protections. We have to make ourselves vulnerable in certain ways if we are to achieve the closeness and connections we require to work with you in new ways. We open ourselves to your hearts and minds and to the forces that flow through them. If we do not do so, if we distance ourselves from your energy, we cannot make the connections we need to make in partnership with you.

Here is where we need your help, for we must draw on your steadiness of heart and spirit to steady ourselves. In a way, you are our protection from the storms of emotion and thought that humanity creates. So you see, to do our work we need you to be like a rock, not unfeeling—no, never that—but strong and grounded and able to give shelter against the emotional and mental winds that blow through your world.

We enfold you in our peace that you may know calm in the midst of these storms, but we need you to enfold us in your peace as well.

At this point, I need to introduce an important element about the Sidhe and their relationship with human beings. R. J. Stewart and John Matthews are two friends and teachers who have years of experience in working with the Sidhe as well as with other subtle beings. Both of them have described the Sidhe as humanity's "cousins". My understanding of information they have shared with me is that at one point in the far distant past, humanity and Sidhe had been a single race or at least shared a common ancestor and thus were kin to each other. At some point, the two had separated, not always amicably, with humanity becoming dominant in the physical realm and the Sidhe moving out of sight into the "hollow hills", a subtle dimension that in some fashion was removed from the material world and yet was still linked to it. Over the centuries, it seems that two main factions evolved within the Sidhe, those who sought reconciliation and collaboration with humanity and those who did not and wanted little or nothing to do with us.

In my working with Mariel and her companions during the creation of the card deck, we connected using a form of telepathy (or what I prefer to think of as *telempathy*, because both thoughts and feelings are exchanged). In this process, there can be "leakage". That is, ideas and images that are not part of the direct conversation but are there as context in the background can "come through" into my mind from time to time. In this case, I became aware of part of this history between us. I came away from several of our conversations with the impression that Mariel represented a faction that was actively seeking to develop collaboration with incarnate humans. At the same time, I also had the impression that there were other Sidhe who had the opposite inclination, who desired to stay as far away as possible from humanity and who even opposed the work of forging new contact.

After her quick visit in the evening, she did return the following day, at which point I was more prepared for her visit. Again, I had the sense that she had come with a purpose, but seeing the state of my body and realizing what I had yet to go through, apparently she set it aside. "There is further work we can do," she said, "but it can wait."

Rather than immediately disappearing, however, she remained, and we held each other in a peaceful energy as she had requested the night before. Thinking about the history of the Sidhe and humanity as I understood it, I took the opportunity to ask her about it. She said:

We are indeed, as you have been told, cousins to each other. Humanity and the Sidhe do share a common ancestor, a primeval race that inhabited this world when it was more energy than matter. The separation between us is often portrayed as a parting of the ways as one part of this race moved more deeply into matter, becoming the humanity you know today, while the other part remained in the realms of energy and spirit becoming the Sidhe. In this story, you become the "fallen ones," while we are the ones who stayed in the Light. Sometimes this split is seen as the result of an ancient conflict or as a need to protect ourselves from an increasingly violent humanity.

There is some truth behind all these images, but our separation is more complex than this. It began not out of conflict but out of exploration and experimentation. The remnants of that event can still be felt in my world as threads of energy going far back into ancestral memory. As you know, we experience time differently from you, so the past, even the far distant past, can under the right circumstances be as close to us as the present.

As images cascaded from her mind into my own, I was reminded of the discovery in the Sixties by our scientists using radio telescopes of the background microwave radiation in the universe. This radiation is seen as a remnant of the Big Bang. Detecting it is like looking back into the past at the very origin of the physical cosmos. In a way under the right circumstances our ancient past is in our present as well.

The events that led to our separation began in innocence and joy. I know! I have felt that past in my heart and know there was no intent to create two separate races. The world was fluid and filled with possibilities. Some of us discovered that we could mold reality into a world of our own imagination and delight, one that allowed us to experiment with the possibilities of our own creation. It was not a parallel world but a part of this one, crafted from imaginal and etheric substance. We even attracted those among the Devic races interested in exploring these possibilities with us who added their own creativity and power.

If this were all there had been to it, it would have been all right, a lovely experiment and diversion from which skills and wisdom would have developed. But there were those who came to prefer this realm of our creation to the one that was evolving and manifesting about us. In this preference the seeds of separation were planted.

Again, her images stimulated a flood of my own thoughts. I thought of the development of cyberspace in our own time, a virtual reality alongside our physical one. Increasingly, more and more people spend more and more time in that world of bytes and bits, images and thoughts, twitters and websites, than they do in the solid world of stone and flesh, plants and animals. I thought of the online worlds such as that of the game *World of Warcraft* in which over fifteen million people around the globe live virtual incarnations as warriors, wizards, thieves, and healers in an evolving fantasy realm. For some people that world is more important and real for them than the one in which their bodies reside. Imagine if at some point the technology of virtual reality and computer processing reached a point where a person could design and live in a fully three-dimensional universe of his or her own creation, filled with the fantasies and products of his or her imagination. How attractive might that be?

Thinking of this gave me a sense of what the Sidhe woman, whose name reminded me of the sparkling freshness of clear water running down a mountain stream, was describing.

This separation did not occur all at once as some calamitous event, though over time there were moments when decisions were made—or forced upon us—that advanced the process beyond the state it had been in. Initially, it was not even seen as a separation but as an extension. We—that is, the ancient race from which you and we stem—saw it as a continuum of experience and incarnation with the world we created at one end and the world that was emerging from Gaia at the other. For a long time it was felt that the whole could be sustained. But as evolution carried us deeper into matter and the physical world became less fluid and more set, it became apparent that this continuum could not last. Choices had to be made.

Although you have it in your mind that we made the choice to separate in order to remain in realms of spirit and Light, this is not true. At least it was not true initially. The crux of the matter then was more that of freedom. As the physical world lost its quick plasticity, the world we had shaped offered more freedom for expression and creativity. Some of us argued that our own evolution would be harmed if we lost this freedom and the possibilities it held and accepted the increasing constraints of physical matter. In the end, it was felt that both would be possible. Some of us would continue creating the realm that we had started and drew cooperation and help from the Devic evolutions to enable us to do so, and others would continue the journey into more solid form and the possibilities of physical matter. At the time, there may have been those who foresaw the consequences of this, but for the most part while those involved in this decision acknowledged that differences would evolve, separation was not considered as a possibility. After all, we were still one people.

Imagine if in our world a movement started to get rid of all computers because they were taking peoples' attention away from the physical world. There would be an outcry against this because we have experienced how computers can augment our creativity and our capacities to do things that would be impossible without them. Yet, it becomes increasingly apparent that there are significant neurological and physical consequences to using computers and other digital devices such as smart-phones and tablets. No one really knows yet just how serious or how negative or positive these consequences may be in the long run to human consciousness. So imagine if our country decided to separate, with everyone to the east of the Mississippi River continuing to use computers, and everyone to the west of that river deciding to minimize or eliminate computer use. Assuming such a thing were possible, we might undertake it not with any idea that in so doing we were creating two new countries. We would assume that people could move freely between these two regions because in essence we were still one country sharing the same continent. Yet over time two very different cultures would emerge. They would share some similarities but they would be different nonetheless. And in time there might evolve the Virtual People and the Land People, each inhabiting their own realm with communication between them growing less and less. This is a simplistic and fantastic image, but it's how I understood what Mariel was telling me.

In effect, the original impulse that brought cosmic humanity into partnership with Gaia included the desire, even the agreement, to accompany the planetary spirit on its journey into matter whatever form this took, even one of greater constriction. If this is where the evolutionary need took us, this is where we would go to learn the lessons or gain the skills that would emerge from such a journey. But there were those who, when faced with the consequences of this descent, questioned the wisdom of it and chose not to proceed, which was their right. At least they wanted to go more slowly in order to be clear about just what those consequences might be.

To continue her story:

But separation did take place, slowly at first but gaining in speed as humanity continued to evolve as a physical species and we…well, we evolved as well, but not in the same way and not as dramatically or rapidly. Or perhaps I should say that the differences between us evolved rapidly over time as you adjusted to your world and we adjusted to ours.

For a long time, there was regular contact and communication between us. But there came a time when our differences began to create conflicts. Humanity was developing a propensity for disconnectedness that shocked many of us; we were unsure how to deal with this, since a sense of connection and wholeness is natural and instinctive to us. Some of us became afraid and lobbied that we retreat from your world, or at the least create boundaries between us. They began to see you as mentally ill, caught up in a sickness induced by too great a descent into matter. Their arguments were compelling, particularly when some of you began to attack some of us.

Understand that this occurred long ago, millennia ago, but it is a cycle that has repeated itself, each time leading us to retreat even more. But there has been a consequence to our retreat for in so doing we have pulled energy out of your world. Or perhaps I should say we have denied our energy to your world, which amounts to the same thing. This was especially so in the beginning as so many of us turned our creative energy away from the evolving world and focused it into the realm that we were shaping in our image. As I said, we did not know all the consequences that would follow for we continued to think of us, you and us together, as a single people in spite of the differences that were growing between us. Without fully realizing what we were doing, we took creative energies out of the world—call it "magic" if you will—and in the process, your world, the physical world, lost some of its lightness. Matter became more restrictive than it might have otherwise, and the humanity that emerged was more deeply enmeshed in it than it might have been. Our ascent became your fall.

Of course, this only intensified and aggravated the differences and the separation between us. And it did something else. We lost some of the strength and—how shall I put this—"groundedness" we might have had had we continued more deeply into matter. We lost a power of will and intensity that you have gained through your struggle with physical matter. We have become too inbred and unable to deal with what is truly other. In this sense, we also have become disconnected, though in a different way from you. We both lost something, and we both became crippled, less overall than we could have been.

Some of us feel the guilt of this. Perhaps to be fair all of us do, though there are many who do not speak of it and have cast it from their minds, accepting the way things are. But there are many like me who know we cannot let things stand as they are but must work to restore the ancient wholeness, for our sake as well as for yours.

I asked her then about the factions I felt within her world and the opposition I imagined she might be facing in starting to work closely with me and other humans. She said:

Opposition is in most cases too strong a word. Even when we differ, there is amicability between us. But you are correct. There are those amongst us who for centuries have turned their backs on humanity and the physical world and who lobby against new attempts at contact. Some fear contamination. They think that through isolation and concentration on our own existence and ways of life that our realm will be protected; it's like avoiding someone who is sick to prevent falling ill with the disease yourself.

Some even regard you with disdain and anger for the harm and imbalance you are bringing to the planet. They feel you should be left to your fate to suffer the consequences of your actions. Many of those who have doubts about our efforts have compassion for you but question the expenditure of energy and wonder if any good or lasting result can be achieved given the state of your world and the resistance of your people to change. And yes, there are some who are fearful of the danger we may personally put ourselves in by engaging with your world in the manner we do.

For as I said, we do need to make ourselves vulnerable if the right connections are to be made.

But the truth is that our worlds are one world, and what affects you affects us and vice versa. Even those who stay in the far reaches of our land will ultimately be affected by what happens to you. So we cannot turn our backs. In the end, there is no protection for any of us save through joining together to pool our efforts in serving the well-being and destiny of the world we share. We need each other. This is the vision that guides those of us who are now actively seeking contact and relationship with your world.

At this point she gave her blessings and left. One thing that struck me about the contact this time was how more solid it felt to me. Mariel felt more present to me, possessing a definite shape and features rather than appearing like swirling ribbons of Light. Like the Sidhe I had met in the forest, she had become more definite and "solid" (if I may use such a word in speaking about a non-physical being) in her approach to the physical world. The telempathic contact was clearer as well and easier for me to sustain. Whatever Mariel had been doing during the months that we had not been in touch, she had improved her ability to be present in the energy field of the material world.

This had been an intense session with many images and feelings flooding into me, more than I've been able to render into words here. I'm sure bits and pieces of insight and understanding will be popping into my consciousness for some time to come. However, right away certain things stood out for me. One was that from her point of view the separation between humanity and Sidhe was not the dramatic story of warfare, conflict and retreat that I had assumed to be true. Such conflicts may indeed have taken place in relatively recent history, but she was telling a story of the far past and of decisions made not in anger, fear, or rejection but out of a burst of creative energy and attachment to its results.

A very similar message came at another time, giving more detail on the history of our two peoples.

Our legends and memory tell us of a time when the physical dimension was more plastic and malleable than it is now, more flowing and responsive to thought. The dimensions you call the "etheric" and the "astral" were also not fully formed, or had not fully separated. So we lived in a world that to you would have been part physical, part etheric, part astral. This world was the bud out of which your world has flowered and is still flowering. It was evident that these layers were separating and becoming more distinct from each other. The call to the humanity that existed then—our common ancestor—was to accompany the world in its differentiation, that is to say, to be able to live in each of the dimensions and indeed to assist in their development. This meant differentiating within ourselves.

But there were those of us who could see that this meant a sacrifice of capabilities we had then, and some of these were unwilling to accept this. They felt they could still serve the world by remaining outside and only partially incarnate, whereas others felt that the call required full participation and immersion in the substance of the world. This was the origin of the split, though there were many complex factors at work. It was not a clear black and white event. There were genuine concerns that certain stellar contacts would be lost as the realms continued to differentiate and the physical became more dense and slow. It was felt, with Gaia's consent, that certain portions of humanity should remain in touch with higher realms and become less embodied whereas others would carry the Light, as it were, as deeply into matter as necessary.

Among these groups, however, were those who went to extremes, those who sought power within matter and those who used the still-fluid, still less-differentiated aspects of the earth to fashion a separate realm, the realm of the Sidhe. The wholeness of human consciousness was sundered. From this arose the challenges that have bedeviled both our races.

As I have said before, our world is not uniform. There are parts of it that are far removed from your own, lost in some ways in its own self-reflection. Other parts of our realm are closer to you and continue to provide service of one kind or another. But you are damaging the fabric of the world in ways that close many of the channels between us. This is what we would help you change, for in doing so you preserve your world but you also preserve ours.

You must understand that when our worlds separated and we separated, there was contact between us for a long time. Still, this separation took magic from both of us. Your world fell more deeply into matter as a result and ours became more insular. We both lost something that might not have been lost had a different solution been found to the challenge of the differentiation and separation of the planes. Yet, though damage was done by this separation, it has also been used for good. For instance, we are in a position to maintain ancient stellar contacts that might have otherwise been lost and we can connect you to those contacts. Imagine if you discovered an island lost in time where dinosaurs still roamed and the land was as it had been millions of years ago. It would be part of your world and yet not part of it. This is what our realm is like. It has evolved, but not as yours has. In some ways we are behind you, and you have much that we need. But in other ways, we are what you need to become.

One thing that was apparent to me was a background feeling of how much the Sidhe need us, in addition to our needing them. She made reference, of course, to the fact that we share one world even though we do so in different ways. But I was taken with her reference to a lack that she felt, that there was some aspect of their consciousness that simply didn't get developed as much as it might have because they retreated into their own realm. My sense was that for all the magic and richness there might be in the world of the Sidhe, it's still essentially a reflection of their own consciousness. The earth we inhabit, however, is the product of and home to a multitude of different consciousnesses at work. It is a place of difference, a place of otherness. We do not live in a realm that only reflects human values, human consciousness and human identity back to us (in spite of our ongoing efforts to change this fact!). We struggle against matter that is not immediately responsive to our thoughts and feelings (though it is responsive in its own way). I cannot imagine a cup of coffee on my desk and have it immediately materialize. If I want coffee, I have to go to the effort of making it. I have to exert will to overcome inertia. And I have to exert at least tolerance if not love to live with all the otherness and difference I encounter daily.

In short, I as an incarnate human being exercise muscles of consciousness that the Sidhe do not. This gives me strengths that they may not have, just as they have strengths I do not. They have learned, for instance, how to fashion connectedness and wholeness, which is not as easy as it sounds.

The bottom line for me is that, however the separation came about between us, we are two species—"cousins"—that need each other and have something to offer to each other in true collaboration and partnership.

CHAPTER TWO
Beyond Nature

I suspect that one reason the Sidhe contacted me is that I was not desiring or seeking such a contact. I've appreciated and honored the work that John Matthews and R. J. Stewart were doing with the Sidhe, but I never felt a need to engage with them myself. My own work in developing Incarnational Spirituality occupied my full attention, to which in recent years I had added new classes teaching subtle perception and collaboration with the subtle worlds. As I said in the Introduction, when Jeremy Berg asked if I'd like to develop a Sidhe card deck, I said no. I didn't feel any attunement to these beings, had little knowledge about them other than what I'd picked up from John and R.J., and in any event, did not need another project on my plate!

Contact, when it came, was therefore a complete surprise. Even afterward, though I was more than happy to collaborate and cooperate, I was concerned that the glamour surrounding the Sidhe would overshadow the other work I was doing.

In the end, though, I was won over by Mariel's presence and began to realize that the work with the Sidhe was not a "sideshow" to everything else I was doing but was an essential piece to a much larger puzzle concerning not only human incarnation but the incarnation of Gaia, the World Soul. As my contact with the Sidhe, including my friend from the forest, developed over the months, I began to want to know more about them so that I might better understand these new allies.

One thing that was clear to me from the outset was that the Sidhe were not subtle beings; that is, they were not denizens of the spiritual and subtle worlds that surround and permeate the earth. I have been in contact with subtle beings all my life, and much of the work I do now concerns ways of understanding and partnering with non-physical beings who live in what I think of as "Earth's second ecology." While subtle beings can vary widely in their nature—the spiritual realms are even more diverse than the physical world—they all have a certain quality or way of impacting my aura or the subtle fields around my physical body.

When Mariel and her companions come to me, though, it's a very different experience. To use a physical metaphor, it's as if I face East to contact a subtle being but I face West to contact the Sidhe. It's difficult to explain, but the difference is very real to me. The Sidhe felt more "full" as if I had to accommodate and hold a wider range of energetic content than I did with a purely subtle being. Imagine dumping a box full of dozens of ping pong balls onto a table and having to corral and hold them all together as they bounce and roll about before any of them fall off the table. There simply was a "lot going on" in the vibrational field of the Sidhe, all of which I needed to embrace to have a good and clear contact. This became easier to do the longer we worked together, as if the ping pong balls became more magnetic and now stuck together on their own accord, making holding them so much easier.

However, I describe it, it took several contacts with Mariel and her companions over a matter of months before I began to feel capable of attuning to her and her world. From what she has said, it took her some time, as well, so we were both learning.

At one point, I asked her about this. What, exactly, were they and where was their world?

You are correct in perceiving that we are not spirits or what you call "subtle beings." We are incarnated like you, though not so deeply into matter as you. The earth has more than one wavelength of physicality. Your wavelength is one of the denser ones, though not the densest. Ours is much less so. Because they are different, our wavelengths can be side by side and we would still not be aware of each other, though at times a form of leakage can occur from one to the other.

Though we are very long-lived by your standards, we are not immortal. We die as well, and when we do, our souls enter the spiritual planes just as yours do. For this reason, we are familiar with what you call the subtle worlds and engage with them just as humans do. And at times, the bridge from our world to yours is through the energy dimensions of the spiritual planes.

At one time we shared the physical world together. As the split occurred between us, we used our affinity with the energies of the earth to move to a different wavelength of planetary life. You moved into a wavelength that was more conditioned and formed, with stronger boundaries between things. Your legends speak of us moving into the "hollow hills" and living within the earth, but this is a metaphor for the most part. We entered into what might be thought of as a "proto-earth," a planetary wavelength that was less conditioned, less formed and thus more easily shaped by our thoughts and imaginations.

In one way, our world would look familiar to you, with landscapes filled with beauty. But this is only our world's "skin". Underneath, it is different, less formed, more fluid, more a condition of thought than of matter. Or more precisely, we live in a world that is the thought of matter that precedes the dense manifestation of matter into the substance you know. Our wavelength is "upstream" from you.

As Mariel attempted to describe this, the image that came to my mind was that of a stem cell in biology. A stem cell is unconditioned; it has the potential of becoming any kind of cell within the body: a nerve cell, a liver cell, a kidney cell, a heart cell. I had a sense that the Sidhe were living in a kind of stem cell aspect of the physical world, one whose plasticity and potential they could shape into different forms as needed but if those forms weren't maintained in some manner, they would dissipate and revert back to the "stem cell" state.

By contrast, we live in a highly conditioned world, one in which, to continue this metaphor, the cells have moved past their stem cell mutability and are locked into particular configurations. Of course, this is just a physical metaphor, so I'm sure it is incomplete and no doubt inaccurate in some ways. Yet, it is the vision that came as I listened to Mariel attempt to describe her world.

In a later message, Mariel explicitly referred to this image which she found in my mind.

Our world is indeed not one of your subtle realms; rather it is an archaic form of the world before these subtle realms had fully differentiated. It is what your physical realm and subtle realms once were in combination. This creates a curious state that gives us access to your physical and subtle realms but not full participation within them, though in a sense they are our subtle realms as well. And the reverse is true. You can have access to us through your subtle dimensions and on rare occasions and in certain areas, through your physical world as well. We are not an "alternate dimension" per se, not another physical earth. We are a more embryonic form of the world you inhabit. You could say we live in the stem cell from which your world has elaborated and differentiated itself. This has frozen us in time. It has preserved in us many of the capabilities and characteristics you think of when you think of us but at a cost, for this world cannot evolve as yours does.

I also remembered something that John Matthews had told me. When he asked his Sidhe contact what his world was like, the reply was "Blue." The Sidhe could not explain it further than that. As Mariel spoke, I suddenly felt I could understand this response, which up till then had seemed mysterious to me. Was this the "archaic form of the world before the subtle realms had fully differentiated"? I don't know. But it seemed to me as if the stem cell state itself was a quality that had no name, no clear definition, so calling it "blue" was as accurate as anything else. I was left with an image of Mariel and other Sidhe living simultaneously in a world that had a discernible landscape and features much like our own—though one that was protean and capable of being shaped by thought—but which also was something else, a state of consciousness and being that was simply a quality or a presence, the "curious state" she mentioned. Like "blue"! In my own mind, I began to think of this place as the "Sidheverse".

In most of the lore, legends, and stories about the Sidhe, they are almost always associated with nature. Sometimes they are thought of as nature spirits themselves. Over the years, I've had lots of contact with various kinds of nature spirits, from very tiny beings that inhabit the materials that make up the structure of our buildings to the spirits of trees to vast beings that overlight entire bioregions. They are a very diverse lot, and I have no doubt that I've only sampled a very few of the many manifestations they can assume.

My contact with the Sidhe, though, has been different. Just as they don't have the "feel" or characteristics of subtle beings, they don't feel like nature spirits to me, either. They certainly have a consciousness that is more attuned to nature than that of the average human being, and I have no doubt many Sidhe have intimate connections with the natural world, just as many humans do. But given that they have a deep affinity with the natural world, they still feel very different from nature spirits to me.

On the occasion of one of her visits, I asked Mariel about this. Here is her reply:

You ask about our relationship to the beings you call the nature spirits and the formative forces of the planet. We are not they, as you have suspected, but their realm intersects with ours in many ways, entwines your world and ours, and holds us together. Remember that our world was initially formed from the physical substance of your own at a time when the material earth was not as dense and solid as it is now. The part that we shaped and made our own had its own etheric and energetic aspects and its own relationship to the formative forces of nature. In those days, it was all one planet, however fluid and protean it may have seemed. The separation did not happen all at once in a mighty cataclysm but over time, though in the end there came events that severed the bonds we shared. But though we are now on a different physical wavelength than you, we continue to share the same subtle realms as you. In the higher worlds of spirit, the planet has not been sundered. It remains whole within the mind and energy of Gaia.

However, from your point of view, we may well seem like nature spirits as we are very attuned to them. And their world is one of our primary bridges into yours. It is often through their realm that we are able to maintain contact and engagement with the physical world.

Sometimes the nature beings are portrayed as our servants. Some of them are willingly responsive to our will, but in actuality they are our partners. There are those amongst us who have blended closely with the great Devas that overlight both our worlds and have become part of their rhythm and service. But they remain Sidhe and not nature spirits, though you may have difficulty detecting the difference. And remember that we can be shape shifters because our outer forms are part of a world whose physicality is less dense and confining than your own.

There is another part to this. Just as the nature spirits can adopt human forms when in contact and communication with human beings, so they can adopt the various forms of Sidhe as well. They can certainly appear to you as one of us, which contributes to the confusion as to who and what we are.

One thing is true. We have not lost the ancient bonds and connectedness to the Soul of this world. We continue to love

Gaia, and through this love, we care about your world and its nature kingdoms as fully as we do our own. We are stewards of life wherever and however it is found, and we would help you become such as well.

It's true that when I am in the presence of the Sidhe, the sense of nature is very strong. I often feel as if I'm in a forest or in a meadow bright with flowers. These are not visual images at all, more like a fragrance or flavor, an impression of a natural environment. In fact, there are times when the Sidhe I've met seem more attuned to nature than the actual nature spirits I've contacted! They come mantled in the poetry of nature, a result no doubt of their own deep attunement to the life and beauty of the world.

CHAPTER THREE
A Sidhe Civilization

I have seen it said that J. R. R. Tolkien in *Lord of the Rings* modeled his tall, stately elves after descriptions of the Sidhe. If this is true, then it's an image that has taken hold. The Sidhe are often seen as horse riding, bow-wielding warriors living in a High Medieval fantasy world, complete with castles and walled towns. As Mariel continued to slowly build the links between us with periodic visitations, she decided to address this. This led to other conversations around the theme of what I call the "Sidhe civilization."

We would like to change your images of us. We are not the forest-dwelling, medieval bow-and spear-carrying warriors you often picture us as being. Oh, you can find such things in our world. Setting aside the thought-forms that are projections of your own thinking and beliefs, there are those of us who delight in re-creating the garb and manner of ancient times. You have such in your own world as well, those who indulge nostalgia for the romantic images of times gone by. And sometimes, if a human's thoughts of us as medieval warriors are particularly strong, we may wear such images for their sakes in order to facilitate contact.

But none of this truly represents who we are. Overall, we are a modern people who have evolved even as you have. We have our equivalents to your cities; we have our technologies. Nevertheless, our people live in diverse ways just as yours do. Not all humans care to use the more advanced technologies available to you, and this is true for us, as well.

Would it surprise you to learn that we are a star-faring people, something your race is only beginning to achieve? Our means of journeying beyond this world are not based on chemistry or physics. We do not depend on the brute force of pushing against gravity to launch small containers filled with the air you breathe and the food you eat. There are pathways of energy and consciousness between the stars which we have always known how to navigate, and in walking them, we have formed bonds with civilizations beyond your own. Such journeys are no less real for being non-physical in their nature.

We are, in other words, a people developed beyond the images in which you hold us.

When she said this, I suddenly had images of a gleaming city with soaring towers and graceful domes, alongside which gleaming spheres of light rose from a spaceport, heading off to the distant planets around other stars. Mariel laughed at this image which, admittedly, rose from a lifetime of reading and enjoying science fiction novels. The following conversation ensued:

Mariel: If you wished to see such a city in our world and such ships rising into space, they could appear for you. But it would just be the way your mind interpreted our reality, projecting what you wished to see to ensure you understood what you were seeing.

David: Then I cannot see what your world is truly like?

Mariel: There are regions in our world that overlap your own in frequency of vibration. In such places if conditions are right, it is possible to step into our world in a physical body, and we can do the same in the other direction. In these regions, you would find a landscape very much like your own for the influence of your land is strong and molds the substance of our world. But if you move away from these borderlands and further into our world, you would have difficulty seeing what is truly there.

David: Why?

Mariel: Think of it this way. In your world, you see the surface of things, which to us is only a small percentage of what is really there. Think of an iceberg which has most of its form below the surface of the water, out of sight from above. You see the solid shape but not its corresponding energy form.

In our world, however, we see the whole object, which includes its energy structure as well as the forms and surfaces that proceed from that structure. So where we might see an entire building, it would look unfinished to you because you would be seeing only part of its nature and structure. You would not see its life or its feeling-sense as part of its form.

David: When I step into a house, I often sense its atmosphere and the energies within it.

Mariel: Yes, but they are feelings and sensations to you. For us, they are substances with which we can build. It is hard to describe because what is substance for us manifests in insubstantial ways for you. It's as if we live in a world of ice but in your world, it all turns to vapor. To see our world, you must look with different eyes than you use in yours. You must look with your heart and with your mind. You must look with all of you.

Another time, Mariel came when I was wondering if the Sidhe had cities in the same way humans do.

We *do* have cities. They are concentrations of creativity, art, culture, and spirit. They are places of joy because those who live there take delight in each other. We have our skyscrapers just as you do, but they are towering structures of thought and energy. They are aspirations made visible. They grow out of the connections and living relationship we have with the spirit of the land on which the city exists.

Our cities and towns have buildings just as yours do, but our buildings do not exist on their own. They are manifestations of living connections. The true city is a core of intent and relationship, often anchored deeply into the earth. They are contracts we have made with the land, and some of them are very ancient. It is hard to explain to you. You live inside structures, but we live inside relationships. The "buildings" arise out of and reflect the nature of these relationships. They can take various appearances which themselves can change quickly if the inhabitants so desire it.

You see, much of what you consider subjective and simply expressions of thought and emotion is for us the substance of our world with which we create and shape the environments in which we live. Like you, we experience that which is inside us and that which is outside, but much of what we see as the "outside" is what is "inside" for you.

Perhaps this will help. You live on the surface of Gaia. We live inside Gaia. This is the true meaning of the legend that we are within the earth. We are not under the ground; we are inside the mind and heart of Gaia, inside the energy of the World Soul. For you, the earth is a surface on which you walk and build. For us, the earth is a life and consciousness within which we reside and out of which we fashion our world, which is a dream of Gaia.

More information about Mariel's people and their civilization came in an answer to a question asked by Jeremy Berg. After the publication of the *Card Deck of the Sidhe*, my contact with the Sidhe diminished for a time. This was not an unusual experience for me, as I've known the same phenomenon in dealing with beings from the subtle worlds. These contacts can come and go, sometimes inexplicably, and you learn that this is OK. They have their own timing.

On the other hand, Jeremy's contact with the Sidhe continued and even increased. In the months that followed, Jeremy began doing workshops on the Sidhe using the card deck as a tool. These were invariably successful, filled with power and inspiration, but Jeremy found he was never able to plan in advance just what would happen, which often left him on the first morning of a workshop still not knowing exactly what he was going to do.

I almost always experience this as well in my own work; the inspiration comes when it's needed, not a moment before. But for Jeremy, this was a new experience, and one that was a bit unsettling at first. He asked me to ask Mariel about it, which I did at the first opportunity that presented itself. Her reply gave a further picture into the nature of her world and civilization.

It is not that we are testing you or are unwilling to be cooperative by making you wait until the moment your workshop starts to begin our collaboration with you. It's just the way that we build things. We do so through attunement in the moment with all the elements and forces that will go into a particular construction, whether it is that of a gathering or that of a building. It's not that we do not plan, it's that our planning is a matter of composing

31

ourselves and attuning to what is needed and what is present, much more than it is of mentally deciding in advance what we are going to do and how to do it. We create in ourselves the seed of what we will manifest. Then in the moment, we allow that seed to unfold and exert its influence, forming its shape as it does so.

If we were to create a building, our architects would find within themselves the living seed of the building. Then they would connect that seed to the environment in which the building will exist. That environment includes the land itself but also other buildings that are nearby and even the people who will use the building. You do something similar, but you do so in advance, creating your plans and blueprints. We are our own blueprints.

Building for us is a relationship, a conversation, an act of growing something organically out of a matrix of possibilities and connections. We site ourselves and hold ourselves in relationship to the land where the building will take place and speak its nature to the world about us. Then we listen to its response. In this way, a living, collaborative image grows within us and around us which becomes a force attracting and shaping what is needed. We mold the substance of our world in this way, and when we are done, a building exists. But it doesn't just sit on the land. It is a flowing, living part of it, a child of the land as much as a child of our own minds and hearts.

It is this creative, conversational approach we bring to our work with you. It is not really improvisational as you understand and use that term, though I understand it may seem so to you. For you, who work differently and build upon plans made in advance, it is improvisational, requiring openness and trust. For us, though, the process is not unplanned but alive and responsive, a process of allowing something to grow organically and in freedom. Yet it doesn't grow unguided. We are the DNA of its growth. We hold the purpose of the life, whether that life is a building or an event constructed in collaboration with you.

In a later visit, Mariel elaborated upon her answer, as both Jeremy and I had further questions about how the Sidhe lived and how they built things (Jeremy was an architect by profession, so this was a very interesting topic for him). To do so, though, she began with a bit of history about the evolution of our two races, beginning with a time when we were all one people.

Greetings. I bring blessings of starfield and earthlight. I appreciate the questions you have brought. I understand that in this collaboration, we seek to know more about each other, and you, rightly so, wish to know more of who we are beyond the legends of folklore. This is as much an experiment for us as for you, so let us see what unfolds.

The seeds of answering your questions lie in the nature of our civilization and, even deeper, in the nature of who you and we are—of who we were in our primal, undivided state. So let me begin there.

We—you and I, or at least our ancestors—came to this world from the stars. We came with varied motives to accomplish different things, but at our core, we came as a formative force. Human and Sidhe are not so far removed from the Devic and Angelic consciousness, and our common ancestor was much closer. You might say we were engineers of the earth. We were—and still are, each of us in our own ways—world-crafters. Our ancestors' coming was both to assist in the shaping and formation of this world and to learn more about our craft in order to heighten our skills.

Our common ancestor was not a hominid creature. It was not a creature of flesh and blood at all, as you know, and it had not yet assumed the appearance that humanity and we now have. This form was dictated as much by planetary circumstances and evolution as by choice and creativity. If you saw our common ancestor, it would resemble little that you know, except perhaps certain devic spirits. It was a being of energy and spirit woven around a latticework of vibrating strings of consciousness.

As she said this, I got a clear image—or as clear an image as is possible of states of being that occupy more than three dimensions! I saw an entity that was roughly spheroid, though not a perfect sphere. It was luminescent and filled with a crisscrossing lattice of what looked like lines of energy connected at various nodal points. Years ago, I wrote that protoplasm was an organic crystal, that it had the property of being able to hold vibrations and energies and create resonance much like a mineral crystal could do but without the rigidity of a mineral. That is what this being reminded me of: an organic, living crystal without the hard angles and edges.

Our ancestor worked with qualities of vibration and frequency that contained the germs of what later became mind and feelings, as well as physical form. The simplest metaphor is that our ancestors worked with sound and spoke or sung into being whatever they were seeking to manifest. Of course, this was not sound in a physical sense, but it is the closest approximation I can find to explain this to you. In a manner of speaking, our ancestor was a living tuning fork, able to produce variable frequencies within itself and in collaboration with others. And it possessed the crystalline property of establishing and maintaining coherency. It was superbly adapted to working in an environment of vibration. After all, the world itself was like a giant vibrating crystal singing in the vastness of the cosmos, and our ancestors came to sing with it in a choir of unfoldment and evolution.

As she presented me with these images, I could not help but think of a laser which is nothing more than light made coherent and focused through the use of a crystal, initially that of a ruby. The sense I had was that our ancestor did something equivalent, though of course on a scale and in a realm far different from the one we inhabit physically. All I can do, at least, is play with metaphors to try and convey what Mariel was telling me, and I'm all too aware of how woefully inadequate some of these metaphors are and how much they may reflect what was in my consciousness more than in hers.

What you must understand is that the capabilities of our ancestor still live within us. You have a word for it: we are *fractals* of that ancient being. Both you and we continue to be formative forces, engineers of earth and crafters of worlds, though we use different techniques to express this. We have both retained this primal identity even as we have evolved our planetary and human forms and even through the separation between us.

In our case, however, we have retained much, though not

all, of our ancestor's capacity to work with vibration and sound and the crystal-like energy matrix of the earth. This is one of the differences between us. It is this capacity that is one of the foundations of our civilization.

The earth is different now than it was when our common ancestor came here to join with the World Soul in its incarnational journey. But in some respects it, too, remains the same. The earth is still a planetary crystal with energies vibrating and coursing along a vast latticework of connections. The phenomena you call the "ley lines" are only an outer representation of this, the manifestation upon the physical of these deeper lines of living energy and consciousness. These physical lines of subtle energy may not be as potent as their inner counterparts, but they are still powerful when used properly.

Perhaps the image of the crystal with its latticework of nodes and connections is a way to illustrate our differences. You took from our common ancestor the capacity to be a node in the lattice, while we took the capacity to form connections. While we know individuality and uniqueness, it is not as intense or as defining an experience for us as it is for you. We do not feel alone in ourselves.

But you are like living standing stones, able to hold your boundaries strongly and within them to hold a variety of other subtle energies as well. You have the capacity to be an alchemical grail in ways that we do not. We can connect to your strength while you can benefit from our openness to flow and to relationships.

Of course, like all images, this one is an oversimplification. It can be restrictive if taken too literally. There are vast individual differences in capacities among us just as there are among you. I cannot speak for all the Sidhe any more than you can speak for all humanity. But certain general statements are permissible.

I said that we were engineers of the earth. We draw directly upon the crystalline matrix of the earth for both power and the capacity of manifestation, both forming what you might term "magic." We build out of our connectedness, just as you build out of your individual visions and efforts. The energy lattice of the earth is constantly vibrating in tune with energies from the sun, moon and stars; the planet sings with the cosmos, and we sing with it. We align ourselves with these vibrations and direct them, guiding them with our thoughts, and in this way, shape the substance of our environment which is much more malleable than your own. When we build, we draw on our own songs but we align them with the songs of the earth. Ours is a technology of telluric vibration and attunement. We are engineers of the music of the planetary sphere and the music of the stars to which it vibrates. We are engineers of song and earth.

Throughout this conversation, images of sound and song, singing and dancing kept coming up. While I think some of these images are literal—in the *Card Deck of the Sidhe*, the Sidhe did refer to themselves as "Dancers"—most of them are not. It's hard to describe just what Mariel showed me. Her reference to themselves as "living tuning forks" seems apt. Watching them at work bringing a building into being, there was much stirring of the energetic atmosphere around them and their work site. There might well have been actual singing going on, but the core of the work was the transmission of an inner vibrating state into the surrounding substance. This could be done in complete silence, at least as far as outer ears are concerned.

What was most clear to me was how attuned these people are to the inner magnetic and vibrational core of our planet. To them the planet really is an energetically ordered and coherent pattern, like a living crystal, and they use its properties to focus energy in a manner reminiscent to me of how we use crystals to focus light in the form of lasers. In this process, they use their own nature—their own inner latticework and matrix of energies—to create resonance to draw out the energies of the earth and then as a lens to focus it.

Perhaps these images give you some sense of the living core of our civilization. I hope so because they are important to answering the questions you have posed me. We work with the energy lattice of the world which has nodes of power and lines of connection. What you must understand, though, is that the creative power we work with is not located either in a node or in the connections but in what emerges from the whole lattice. This is the heart song of the earth that carries the power of life and

36

potential for all life on this planet. This, for us, is the presence of the World Soul that you call Gaia.

When we were part of your physical world and the separation between us had not advanced very far, we built edifices of power and light over many of the planetary nodes. These are not the standing stones and stone circles with which you are familiar. They were made of more etheric substance, but they set a pattern from which the practice of creating standing stones and stone circles emerged at a later date. And some of these monoliths were created by your people on the same sites where we had built our own. This was done partly to connect with us, but primarily because these places are where the planetary nodes are.

There is an irony here. Originally these places of power which we built—and in those days we were still largely one people—were like whirlpools of energy, vast and potent fields of force. There were individuals who were skilled in weaving these energies and connecting them with distant points, but they depended on the complementary skill of those who could stand, hold, and contain the energies in a manner that made them accessible and useful to us.

These individuals were truly living standing stones. Together, the singers, the dancers, and the holders—those who could stand and bear the weight of the forces within themselves—turned the raw power of planetary energy into energies we could use and with which we could create. As you have surmised, we could use this energy to transport ourselves instantly from one node to another on the earth. And we could use it to bring vitality to the surface to enhance the life of everything in the region of the node, working with the devic forces in that area.

As I said, our technology was—and still is—based on this relationship with the living earth. But when the separation occurred, the power of this technology was withdrawn; we took it into our world and in the process drained your world of some of its vitality, precipitating a deeper fall into matter than had been intended.

However, the crystal matrix of planetary forces is still as available to you as it is to us. As we who became Sidhe retreated and you who became human expanded upon the world, you carried with you the memory of the telluric technology of node, connection, and flow, shaped by song and dance and ritual. Guided by this memory, you discovered new ways to tap the sites of power. The practice of building stone circles and erecting standing stones began. What once was done by a person became embodied in stone. This worked as long as the stones were alive, but as the descent into matter continued, and much more importantly, as you lost the ability to form connections with the livingness of matter, the stones have become just what you see today, dormant and in some cases truly dead to the ancient powers.

In some of the places where stone circles or standing stones exist, our own shrines and edifices of power are still there as well, in some cases dormant, in other cases not, but all existing in our world. Some look like your circles of standing stones, others do not. But none are as powerful as they once were because we have lost some of the power of standing and holding. This is one reason we wish to reconnect with you, for together we are the complements that create a whole, living matrix, one capable of singing the energies of the earth back into the planes of physical matter and into our world as well.

This is why we come to you. But first things first. Your world is truly not yet ready for the technology we could bring. It is not just that humanity is unready, though that is largely true. It is also that the etheric planes of the earth are cloudy and polluted; the lens has imperfections in it, so to speak, that can distort the forces that are released. There is much to be done before either of us can safely recapture what once was.

Blessings of starfield and earthlight to you and blessings of the Song of Life as well. May it sing always in your hearts.

On another visit, I made a comment about the Sidhe being part of the Faerie realm. Mariel had an immediate and amused response:

What is Faerie? It is a word you humans have conceived to cover a wide variety of phenomenon, often anything you don't understand or that seems "magical" to you. If by "Faerie" you mean a collection of realms that are truly part of the physical world but on a different wavelength or vibration from the one you inhabit and thus are normally invisible to you, then yes, we are Faerie beings. But if you mean those beings who are Children of Gaia, then we are not Faerie for we, like you, are children of the stars.

This was all she said at the time, but over a year later, she came back to this topic and elaborated upon it. This information comes later in this book as it was part of a discussion that took place in the Sidhe class that is the subject of Part II. However, the next time she came, I pursued this topic a bit by asking about the Faerie Queen and King. Given what Mariel had already said, I was asking this partly in humor based on long-standing human archetypes about the "Faerie Court", an idea often found in fantasy literature from Shakespeare down to modern authors. Mariel, who always had a sense of joy and humor about her, recognized the jest behind my intent but chose to answer me seriously.

Ah, yes, the Faerie Queen and King! Do they exist? Would you accept my saying yes and no? Remember that though we are your kin and part of the larger domain of humanity, we are not the same as you. Our minds are structured differently than yours. For example, we naturally experience telepathy or a mental empathy and contact with each other. This means that the challenges and possibilities of communication and coordination when we congregate and work together in groups are different for us than for you. We have less need for what you call "command and control" as in many ways we instinctively know how to coordinate and work together.

It's not that we experience oneness or that we have a shared mind, a hive mind as you might put it; we are still aware and respectful of each other as individuals. But we can express greater coherency in our efforts than you do without the need for hierarchies or structures. So you could say we can manifest a "team mind," more than a mind requiring ranks and hierarchies in order to accomplish complex tasks.

For this reason, we don't have government in the same way you do—there is no need among us. But this doesn't mean that we don't have leaders or those who supervise or overlight large and complex tasks. We do. For the most part, they are not chosen or elected as much as they arise out of the task itself as those most fitted to be in a leadership position. And we have councils, gatherings of interested or responsible individuals who take on tasks of planning, oversight, and coordination when necessary.

We also have what you might think of as Elders, not necessarily those who are oldest or most experienced, though this can be the case as well, but those who obviously embody high degrees of wisdom. You might think of them as "Soul Elders" rather than "Time Elders." In this regard, our social structure is probably most similar to any human system in which deference and honor are paid to elders and their guidance is sought.

But like your Americas, we have as well a high regard for individuality and uniqueness, so there is no pressure to conform for the most part, though in any group of individuals you will find a certain tide of energy and thought arising from the majority that can sweep others along.

However, having said this, it is also true that we have a King and Queen. They are not "royalty" in the human sense, and there is no Court as such, though there are those whose function and lives are to serve and act in close proximity to our "Highnesses." Our King and Queen are more like personifications of all that is highest and most noble among the Sidhe. They are the embodiments of our dreams and visions as well as our memories; they are the manifestations of where we have come from but also of where we hope to go. In your terms, they might be considered the Angels or Devas of our race. In a manner of speaking, they are not truly Sidhe yet they are the essence of the Sidhe, if this makes sense to you. They are not two individual Sidhe elevated above other Sidhe and given greater rank. They are the embodiment of the spiritual essence of our race.

They are not abstractions, however, but very real presences, and one can visit and commune with them. They do not rule in a human sense, but they are powerful influences and definitely help shape who we are and where we are going. But unlike a human king or queen, they can inhabit any of us. That is, any one of us at any time can be infused with the presence of our King and Queen and in that moment become "kingly" or "queenly."

This is not an act of possession or of one spirit entering the body of another. It is that the essence of Sidheness is heightened in us in a unique way, usually appropriate to the situation. Do you understand? If the Queen overlights me, then a "Queenly" aspect in me is heightened and drawn to the surface, and in this moment, I become a "Faery Queen" within the context in which I am working. I know you felt this in me when we first met and wondered for a time if I might not be the Queen of the Faeries. In that moment, I was indeed that Personage in order to have the power to make our initial contact. But when this was achieved, this Presence withdrew. When the need for that heightening passed, then I was simply myself.

Unlike in the human world, we do not have "royalty" and "peasants." In a real way, royal blood in the form of a spirit and life connection with our King and Queen flows through all of us. But we are certainly of different levels of accomplishment, wisdom, and insight, and some of us are better able to embody and hold the presence and essence of the King and Queen within themselves than others.

Do we have institutions of government? Again, the answer is yes and no. We do not have anything like you have. But there are those among us who are tasked with the long-term wellbeing of our race and who perform functions of vision, coordination, and planning akin to what you would find in your governments. They form a structure together that is long-lasting. But like all things in our world, this structure is more fluid and mutable than fixed, able to change and respond when necessary.

This is not to say we do not have among us, as you do, those who seek power for its sake or who think themselves of higher rank than others; after all, we are only Sidhe [and this was said with a certain twinkle of humor since it was an obvious play on our words, "well, we're only human!" —David]! We have our challenges and our challenging individuals. But we do not have the kind of corruption or power lust you have since our structure of mind, as I said, does not lend itself to it. Still, there have been exceptions.

So the King and Queen of the Sidhe are real, but how you think and write about them are mainly humanly created imaginative constructs, projections of your own images of rulership and government.

Blessings as always, and blessings from our Highnesses!

CHAPTER FOUR
Collaboration

When the work on the *Card Deck of the Sidhe* was finished in the summer of 2011, I thought that my involvement with the Sidhe was over. But as I've been describing, throughout the next two years, contact with Mariel continued and after a hiatus began to increase. I began to realize that the card deck was only a part of a larger agenda. I asked her about this on one of her visits.

We do not have a master plan but yes, we do have a larger purpose in mind. I and my colleagues are one of several groups exploring the possibilities of collaboration between your people and mine. This is an experimental work. We are "testing the waters", as you would say. We are exploring what can unfold between us. Much is unknown, which is why we cannot plan. In fact, we are not planners in the same way you are; we are sensitive to what is present and thus what may unfold in the moment and work to aid that unfoldment. So we build the field of energy between us and observe to see what will emerge.

However, we are not arbitrary in this process. We are aware that things unfold step by step and work accordingly. The card deck was a first step. Depending on the results of its existence and use in your world, we will see what other steps become available.

Over the years, my work with the subtle worlds has been all about forming alliances and collaborations with subtle beings. I believe the universe basically operates from a partnership cosmology fueled by love. If we are entering a new cycle in planetary evolution, it is one I believe is characterized by connection and cooperation in the interests of creating wholeness. So it made sense to me that the Sidhe would be seeking collaboration with human beings. However, I wanted to explore further with Mariel just what this might mean. The theme of collaboration became a thread that ran through several of her conversations with me over several months.

There are many reasons why collaboration between us is important. For one thing, we are kin. The same ancestral spirit is in you that is in us. It is time for our family to be reconciled and reconnected so that we may be whole again. The world needs our wholeness, particularly at this time.

Also, we need each other. You understand the incarnational process more deeply that we do. By entering the world as you have, you have touched the sacredness within matter and within the act of uniting with it. Though we know the joy and presence of the Sacred, we do not know this deeper aspect. You have depths from which we may draw.

At the same time, we have knowledge of life and skills of weaving and blending living energies together that you have lost. You are sensitive to the individuality of things, but we are aware of the wholeness of things. You have the power of synthesis, but we have the power of connection. Both create wholeness.

We know the earth and nature in ways that you have forgotten. Our sensitivity and knowledge can be useful to you as you face the challenges you have created. But you can act in the world in ways we cannot.

There are deeper issues at work as well that I will discuss later. It is enough for now to appreciate that we need each other and have gifts to exchange that will benefit us both and the world we share. Perhaps most excitingly, neither of us can say just what may emerge as we learn to work and blend together!

You must understand that we, like you, are a large and varied people. You might say we have "races" and "ethnicities" of consciousness and attitude. They are not as fixed into form as your different racial characteristics are but they can demarcate us as fully as your differences do you. Therefore, anything I say of a general nature about the Sidhe must be understood in this context. I do not speak for all the Sidhe, anymore than you can speak for all humans.

Not all Sidhe feel or desire a connection with humanity. Some of us are far removed from the human norm in ways that make communication or relationship difficult, even if they wished. Others are close to your world but are caught within the thought-forms you create of us.

44

But there are those among us who have through the centuries known of our kinship and of what we can be together. They have held the ideal of our eventual wholeness. These are the Sidhe who believe in and are committed to collaboration and partnership and to the unknown possibilities that may emerge between us.

I am one of them.

Another time she had this to say:

There are many ways to understand and to connect with the Sidhe. We are as diverse a race as you are. I know you are curious about who we are and what our lives and culture are like. There is no reason for you not to have this information, and each of you can learn more about us in your own way through your own attunements. But I and my companions are a working team that wishes to relate to you in a particular way. In the context of our teamwork, this cultural information can be a distraction, useful only if it strengthens our connection and collaboration.

Our interest is less in instructing you about who we are and more about alerting you to the nature that unites us and makes you one with us and we with you. For our desire is for you to know the inner qualities you share with us—what you might call the "Sidhe Within"—so that you become more whole in your own lives and can better tap your own creative capacities. We want you as our dance partners because in this dance the new world will emerge. You don't have to know our culture to dance with us, but you do need to know the steps of the dance. The world calls for you to do so.

This was another message on the same theme:

For all that you have journeyed into matter and faced the challenges that it has posed, you still carry within you the presence of our ancient, common ancestor. You carry its potential as a creator of wholeness. This is what we wish to awaken in you. We want you to remember who and what you are, the family to which you belong.

Our races have grown and developed since we shared that

common identity; there is no going back to what was, nor would we wish to. But we are both incomplete. The potential of our mutual origin lies in both of us but neither of us can fully access it without the collaboration of the other. It takes two halves to bring out the whole.

So we come to you not simply to tell you of our existence or to give you arcane knowledge or share the wonders of our realm. We come in the hope that by sharing our presence together we can both incarnate the wholeness that is within us. We will discover the human in us, you will discover the Sidhe in you. In so doing, we will both discover the beginnings of a new world for us all.

At different times, Mariel would express concern about the power the images that we held about the Sidhe and about ourselves had to interfere with connection and cooperation between us. Some of this concern I felt from her in the form of "leakage" or thoughts that would be present in the background when she was discussing something else. But on one occasion, she addressed this matter directly.

It's important that you are very careful in how you think of us and in the thought-forms you accept and energize. This is why we have asked you not to form images of us, as with the card deck that was our initial project. None of your images of us are accurate enough, or perhaps I should say, up to date enough to fully serve you or us in this enterprise between us.

In particular, I would like you not to see us as having a special kinship with nature when compared to yourselves. This is an old image, and as I have said previously, we are not nature spirits, though we have a close association with them. But you have powerful and important connections to nature as well. You need to appreciate your own connections in this regard—which are different from our own—and not make attunement to nature a line of differentiation between us.

We may be aware of the wholeness of Nature and act on its behalf more than you do in your culture, and we can offer important perspectives out of our awareness, but we do not wish you to deny or fail to see your own sensitivity to this wholeness.

How can you practice and enhance it if you deny it to yourselves or credit it only to us? To say we are the champions of nature and you are not is a false and limiting image and only obstructs our work together. Oneness with Nature is as much a part of who you are as it is a part of who we are. All you need to do is remember this and draw it out into the light of your consciousness. If we can inspire and help you to do so, this is what we would wish, but do not make us an obstacle to this process by creating divisions and thought-forms where none need exist.

Later, she put it very succinctly:

To find the "Sidhe" within yourselves, find the fullness of your human spirit within yourself.

On the other hand, Mariel did not entirely dismiss the usefulness and power of certain thought-forms and imaginal creations that humans have produced. My Christmas 2013 issue of my esoteric journal, Views from the Borderland, focused on the history and image of Santa Claus as an expression of a deep spiritual truth. While writing this, Mariel appeared and I took the opportunity to ask her what she thought of Santa Claus.

Santa Claus? Yes, we know him well. How could we not since in your folklore and stories, you so often attribute him to our realm? You see him as a magical being, perhaps one of the Faery realm, perhaps a Sidhe, a being like us. And in some ways, he is like us, a being of joy who has the elements of the trickster about him even as he works wonders to bring happiness on earth.

Sometimes there are those of us who take on the appearance of Santa Claus and enter your etheric realm as a means of participating in your world at this time of celebration. Those who do, do so in a spirit of fun. But others of us are intrigued and see in this being your longing to reawaken your own magic. After all, in your legends Santa is often portrayed as a human being who becomes like one of us, an immortal member of the Faery realm.

Santa seems to connect you in mysterious ways to the common ancestor we once shared. So it seems to us that Santa is both a memory of who you once were when you claimed and knew your own spirit's magic and a hope for who you can become once more as a being of generosity, love and connection with the natural world.

So indeed we celebrate Santa Claus and honor his presence among you both as thought-form and as spirit. He links you with us, and this, to us, is a link to foster.

Do we celebrate as you do at this time of year? Yes, but for different reasons. Remember that our world is different from yours in significant ways. We do not have a procession of seasons as you do but can create the seasonal effect and environment that we wish. If we wish summer, we can manifest it so or if we wish winter, we can do this as well. There are some natural limits upon our ability to do so, but on the whole, what I have said is true. So we do not have a cycle in which days grow longer or shorter or in which the Light increases or decreases.

But we do celebrate the gift of Light and its presence amongst us. And we celebrate the powers of growth and vitality in a manner equivalent to your summer solstice, and we celebrate the powers of silence and contemplation and renewal as reflected in your wintertime. And we celebrate our joining with the earth, a celebration we can share with you for we both descend from the common ancestor who first came to this world from the starry dimensions.

When you celebrate, you can certainly invite us to join you, and we will. For in all celebrations there is joy, and it is joy that links us together, joy that defines who we are, we in our realm and you in yours. We remember this joy, but you often forget. So any opportunity we have to remind you is a blessing to us and, we hope, a blessing to you.

At this time, largely through the personage of Santa Claus, you celebrate the presence of magic in your world—or at least your hope for magic—and this resonates with us. So we are able to draw closer to your world and affairs. Invite us in, and we will share our joy with you and remind you of the magic within your lives.

Another issue that came up several times was the actual dynamics of contact between Sidhe and human. It was reflected in my own experience in the way that Mariel had first seemed shapeless to me, no more than swirling mist and ribbons of light. Later, as the contact developed, she took on a more consistent form. But it was not always easy for me to tell how much of this form was a projection from my consciousness and how much was actually her own person and appearance.

This challenge has to do with the difference in how matter behaves in their world from ours. Trying to comprehend and translate what Mariel was attempting to show me and tell me, I fell back on using words like "fluid" and "fluidity" as well as "fixed" and "fixity". Neither of these are quite adequate, but I hope they convey the sense of what she was trying to communicate. Here are those conversations.

We are viewed as fluid beings, shape-shifters, and in comparison with you, this is true. But it is also a condition of the differences between the wavelengths of our worlds and the energetic threshold between us. It is an intermediate state. In our own realm, we are solid and can be as fixed as you. The matter of our world has the same integrity as yours in being what it is, but it is more malleable and directly responsive to our thoughts and feelings than your matter is to you. Our matter holds within itself closer to the surface the possibilities of different states of being; it can easily shift from one state to another. You could say that the atoms of our world are themselves shape-shifters, occupying multiple states of energy and possibility at once.

Your matter has this same inherent potential of possessing multiple states at once, but in fact, it manifests in what we would view as a collapsed state. It collapses into and expresses one possible state at a time, which gives it a forcefulness our matter doesn't have. Perhaps *definiteness* is a better term. Your atoms are definitely in a particular state whereas ours are provisionally in one state but other states are closely accessible. It's this that makes our matter so willing to change. Because you are native to this state of matter, your own thoughts and feelings, mediated through the substance of your material brains, have this definiteness or forcefulness to them as well.

Therefore, when we approach your world, both its physical

energy and the energy of your consciousnesses impact us with this forcefulness, causing us to lose our definition and become more flowing.

It's as if the pressure and force of your world heats us and renders us liquid, like melting wax so you can pour it into a mold. This is one reason we've asked you not to form images and thought-forms about us and about what we look like and who we are, for it's too easy for some of us, approaching your state of being, to flow into those thought-forms and become trapped in them while we are interacting with you.

This fluid, intermediate state is a natural phenomenon brought about by the differences in energy between your state of being and ours. It's not that we cannot hold our form when we are with you, but it takes effort and training—we must be clear who we are, and this clarity can be challenged by the forcefulness of your imaginations of who you think we are.

There are Sidhe who are close to your world but who have achieved this closeness by surrendering to the thought-forms you have built up of us—and this is even more true today than in earlier times with the many representations of us in your literature and stories. There are strong thought-forms in your culture about the realms of Faery and of the Elves and the Courts of the Sidhe. We can use these thought-forms and at times we do delight in doing so, much as you would delight in putting on costumes and pretending you are someone else in another time, another place. But they do not necessarily advance the cause of our collaboration and blending.

In the terms of the cards which we presented to you, you are like the standing stones, for you embody the solidity of your world that is different from our own, and by comparison to us when we approach you, you can be very stone-like. There is a benefit to this for you and for us, but also a challenge.

We, on the other hand, are the Dancers that can move among the stones, felt as presence but not given a specific form. For you see, we are stones, too, in our world, and if we bring our stone-ness into your stone circle, we will clash. We will bump up against each other. So we melt and flow and move amongst you in fluid, misty ways, like fog around the stones.

50

What is not apparent to you, though, is that this relationship works both ways. For you to truly enter our world, you must become the dancers that weave around us as stones. The cards mirror a reality in both worlds, for we are both stones and dancers. You must surrender your fixity and melt into a more fluid part of yourselves, becoming more Sidhe-like in this regard. But this fluidity doesn't define who you are any more than it defines who we are. It is a capacity that we both have that can enable us to melt into each other.

I say this because to define us as flowing and fluid-like creatures can become yet another thought form limiting you to one conception of who and what we are—as well as potentially limiting how you think of yourselves if you only see yourselves as fixed and solid. You are standing stones to us, but we can be standing stones to you as well, and we can both be dancers together.

At a later visit, Mariel returned to this theme which was apparently important to her.

We are people like yourselves. In our world and in ourselves, we have both fixed and fluid aspects, "bone and blood" as you would say. Our world is different in that it is more malleable and responsive to the impressions of our consciousnesses; our intentions can directly affect the shape of the world around us. But even here there are limits. We are not unbounded in this capacity, nor does our world wholly lack any consistency or fixed substance. So the difference between our worlds is one of degree.

Your world has inertia and boundaries, but ours does as well. Let me use a metaphor to make this clear. If we were both ocean-dwellers, our world is closer to the surface where the pressure of such inertia and boundaries is less while your world is towards the bottom of the sea (though not at the bottom, I assure you) where the pressure is much greater. Unless we take measures, our bodies tend to dissolve as we approach your state of being, as I described; we become more flowing in contrast, which helps us adapt to you, but as I said, can also be a trap if we become enclosed in your fixed images.

Your question is what happens to you when you approach our state of being, and how might you successfully do so in order to better commune with us? Just as a creature of the deep ocean may expand as it enters regions of lesser pressure, so you can feel expanded when we are near and you are drawn into our state of being. In this condition, you can lose your boundaries, too, and your sense of self, becoming "high" and ungrounded and, yes, more subject to illusion and glamour.

It is not that we project such glamour necessarily, though there are those of us who do or who take advantage of your compromised state in this regard. This is a misconception. It is that your subtle senses expand in their sensitivity, making you more susceptible to what you perceive as the beauty and grace and the usually harmonious conditions of our realm. You can become intoxicated, which can become fun for some of our kind to observe but it does not help foster partnership! In other words, our ordinary world seems glamorous and extraordinary to you because you are temporarily expanded beyond your boundaries and thus less capable of discernment.

So the first step in dealing with us is to be well-grounded in who you are and in your own identity, as this can give you the capacity to hold your boundaries and see through the glamour which is as much a product of your own heightened but ungrounded perception as it is of our doing.

You are already fluid beings in your own way when you choose to be, and you express your fluidity in your capacity to adapt to changes, particularly unexpected ones. You yourself have a phrase for it: "going with the flow." So in dealing with us, you must strengthen this adaptability. Find the part of you that knows how to be resilient and adaptable. Think of when circumstances forced you to step out of the boundaries of the familiar and the known and adapt to new conditions. How did you do this? Who did you become in that moment to be adaptable to what was happening around you or to you?

This is your fluid self, but it's a "grounded fluidity", if you understand my meaning. When you successfully adapt to and flow with changing circumstances in your life, you are fluid in a grounded, practical way, one that is connected to what is happening and to your environment. You are not simply swept away.

It's this state of mind and being that we would encourage you to enter when you connect with us. It's a state of letting go of your fixed thought forms of how things should be, of what you should be like, and of what we should be like so that you are more adaptable to what is actually around you. Be open. Be imaginative. Be loving. But trust in yourself and be sure of who you are, as well. It isn't so much that you exchange fluidity for fixity but that you are flexible, able to be fluid and fixed in new ways.

I hope that this is helpful. Blessings as always from me and my kind.

Interestingly, one reason for collaboration between Sidhe and human that she did not bring up was as a response to the ecological challenges we are facing in the world, the most alarming of which is climate change. Given the attunement and sensitivity of the Sidhe to nature and wholeness, I think I was expecting her to give some warning or make some pronouncement about our relationship to nature or how badly we are treating the earth and what we should do about it. When this didn't come, I decided to bring up the issue myself and see what she had to say. This was her response:

Do you need more warnings? Do you need your eyes opened to what is happening in your world? I think not. In any event, it is not my purpose or task to bring you apocalyptic messages. Others are doing this and will continue to do this. My work with you is different. We have different objectives.

But as you have asked, I will say this. Do you fear the collapse of your civilization as it proves inadequate to the changes happening in the world? Far better to fear the collapse of hope. Far better to fear the collapse of joy. Far better to be alarmed at the collapse of imagination and creativity. For these are the qualities that you need to change your direction in the world. The loss of your coastlines to a rising sea is nothing compared to the loss of your capacity to love and to find wholeness within yourself and within your world.

Humans are not facing challenges of ecology. You are facing challenges of psychology. Your inner climate is wracked with storms of fear and anger, hatred and revenge. This is where change must happen. It is how you think of yourselves that must transform. What can you do to change your inner climate?

Yes, nature needs your help. Yes, the world needs your concern, your awareness, your love, your support. Yes, you are threatened. But what truly threatens you are outworn thought-forms of who you are. You do not see the wholeness of life in the world, and because of this, you do not see the wholeness of life within yourselves.

We can help with this. More importantly, you, each of you, can help with this. Choose to see the world as a living presence. Choose to see the power of love within yourself. Change your inner climate and you will find your way to a new world. Stay as you are, and a new world will still be upon you, but it will not be to your liking...or to ours.

This is the nature of my work with you. My companions and I seek to change the climate of your lives. Then we can truly be partners.

Is this warning enough? Is this hope enough?

In an earlier conversation, when discussing collaboration between the Sidhe and humanity, Mariel had said, "There are deeper issues at work as well that I will discuss later. " Eventually, that "later" arrived, and this is what she had to say:

There is a larger reality that draws us together, your people and mine. It is a need to make possible a potential that can emerge between us. It is a mystery that we also wish to understand more fully, so I cannot fully explain it to you. But it goes beyond simple collaboration or cooperation between us and arises from the depths of our shared ancestry. It is a matter that deals with your future evolution and ours and the evolution of Gaia herself.

There is a wholeness that we once knew together and that has remained as a seed within your race and mine that is now asserting itself and seeking to manifest anew. It does so in response to a need and an urge within Gaia herself to achieve a new level of coherency and integration within her own being.

Not all of the Sidhe are aware of this, and not all of the Sidhe who desire greater collaboration with human beings perceive this. But it is a vision to which I respond and which informs the relationship that I and my colleagues have with you.

Even though we split into two peoples, there is a higher level of consciousness in which we are still whole and have always been whole, a single race. This higher level is exerting itself to bring its divided and scattered parts back together. This goes beyond collaboration as an exercise of intentional cooperation and becomes instead something more akin to a metabolic process, the assertion of life to reinstate an organic integrity. Thus, in the work we're exploring with you, we're not so much forming a partnership as we are unfolding a larger wholeness of which we are both been (and have always been) a part.

Of course, collaboration itself is a large step and in many instances a first step for both of our peoples, but behind and beyond it is this deeper mystery of emergence. It is tied directly to the emergence of a new coherency and wholeness within the energetic structure of the planet as a whole. In a way, what is seeking emergence is what you might call a new planetary subtle body.

It is difficult for me to fully convey how we see and experience this, in part because your human concept of the world is too influenced by your concept of a physical planet in space separate from other planets, separate from the sun and moon, separate from the stars.

To us, all these celestial bodies are living beings who form a most intricate and intimate web of connection and influence, of which Gaia is a part. But now the pattern and structure of this "web" is changing. Many of the relationships which Gaia has with its cosmic environment and family are changing, and we—you and I—are part of this change.

This web of stellar relationships and connections is embedded in what you call the subtle fields of the planet; to some extent, it structures these fields in the way bones structure your body. As this web changes, the subtle field changes. Gaia gains a new "subtle body," and as she does so, you and we do as well.

This new subtle body enhances the connectedness and communion Gaia has with her cosmic environment. It means that more energies from the stars will flow into this world, and the living energy of the planet will in turn flow more freely into the cosmos. All the environments of consciousness held within the planetary matrix, which includes your world and mine, are being energetically heightened in one way or another. All planetary life must adapt.

What I wish to explain as best I can is that the spirit of our ancient, common ancestor already possessed deep connections and attunement to the stellar energies now flowing into the earth. It is a seed for the new subtle bodies that seek emergence in and around us. But it is a seed we both carry. It will unfold more easily in each of us if we can help it to unfold together. It will not be easy since we are now different from each other, but the larger wholeness that holds both of us within itself is a resource upon which we can draw if we can connect to each other in partnership.

The whole issue of collaboration with the Sidhe became a major topic in a class that Jeremy, Mariel, and I held online in April and May of 2014. The material from this class is what forms the rest of this book beginning with Part II.

CHAPTER FIVE
The Mantle

My esoteric journal, *Views from the Borderland*, is sent to subscribers four times a year. It's not an online publication but an old-fashioned, hardcopy print document, so it's sent through the mails. However, twice I year, I sponsor a subscribers' Forum online which gives everyone who reads the journal a chance to interact with me, ask me questions, and enter into discussion with me and others who participate. Over the years, these Forums have developed into a growing online community of like-minded people who support each other in their spiritual journeys. They've become a safe place to share experiences, stories, and questions, all in the interest of helping each other gain deeper understanding of the subtle and spiritual realms of the Earth and how to effectively engage with them in partnership.

In the summer of 2012, I devoted one of the journals to my irregular but nonetheless ongoing contact with Mariel and the Sidhe. When it came time to have our Forum in October, that issue and the topic of the Sidhe quickly became the most popular and dynamic subjects under discussion. In the process, a remarkable field of energy built up among the participants, and Mariel and her companions took full advantage of its presence.

I had been feeling as the year progressed that after the Sidhe deck there was more to come. I've already mentioned that I felt Mariel had some agenda, even though she denied planning things out in advance. There was something that they hoped to be able to do, though I had no clue what it might be. Then, as the energy built in the Forum, over the last couple of days, the penny finally dropped.

I was sitting on my sofa reading when I became aware of Mariel's presence along with that of her two companions. At first no words were spoken. Instead I had an image of a circle of large, ancient but beautiful standing stones. I had the strong sense that this circle was a portal between worlds, a meeting place and threshold. But it was more than that, more than just a doorway. It was also a force or an activity; it was a presence that created and held unity and wholeness between the worlds—really between all differences. To stand in the middle of this circle of stones was to stand in the midst of this presence of wholeness

Then Mariel spoke:

"We Sidhe are the Guardians of the Circles, of all they contain and all they connect. These Circles stood like great sentinels and places of power upon the land. But now it is time for these Circles to live in the hearts and lives of people, your people. For this to happen, we wish to share our mantle of Guardianship with anyone who can stand in the Circle of his or her own heart as we have stood in the Circles upon the Land. It is time for the Circle upon the land to become the Circle within the body, within the heart, within the mind. If you choose to stand in this place and accept the mantle of its Presence, guard it well as we have done and be a Circle for your world."

At this point, just as had happened with the card deck, Mariel outlined a very simple exercise for me to offer to the people gathered in the online Forum. As she did so, I felt that she and the Sidhe with her were passing on a profound gift. They were offering to share with us a lineage that they have held for millennia. I realized that the card deck, with its "portable Stone Circle", was a prelude to this, that it created a foundation and a tool that could be used in passing on this mantle. In its way, this exercise was a further embodiment of the project which Mariel and her companions were working upon.

In writing about this now, it's hard to capture what I experienced that afternoon. The whole living room seemed to fill with a presence that felt deep and redolent with earth light and star light. I could easily feel great standing stones surrounding and holding the house, and it seemed that it was the stones themselves that were communicating wordlessly with me even as Mariel offered her thoughts and suggestions.

Some months later, Jeremy wrote and published a delightful fairy tale for children and young people. Jeremy is a natural storyteller, and this one of his best. Titled *Faerie Blood*, it is illustrated with his own paintings in the same style as he used for the cards in the *Card Deck of the Sidhe*. Seeing one of the paintings in the book, it took my breath away because for me, it totally captured the feeling I had that afternoon as the great stones filled my living room and Mariel outlined the Guardian Mantle exercise. The star at the center of the stone circle was, for me, the Light at the heart of the exercise, the light of the mantle of wholeness.

It's a very simple exercise, but it carried a lot of power with it. As I thought about it and felt into it prior to sharing with the Forum, I had the sense that it actually was not an exercise at all but a covenant, a form of initiation and commitment. As with all such things, a person needs to be willing to enter into such a covenant and initiation; it can never be forced. And for it to "take," it has to be entered into in right timing when a person is ready for its implications and consequences and with a spirit that understands what it is taking on.

I confess at first I experienced some reluctance in posting the exercise in the Forum. It felt too powerful to me, and I was concerned there might be repercussions. But Mariel assured me all would be fine and to have confidence both in the people who participated in the Forum as well as in myself.

By then, I had truly come to trust my Sidhe allies and felt they would not have presented this invitation and gift in this way were it not appropriate.

Here is what I wrote on the Forum as I presented the exercise. I explained what had happened just as I have explained it to you above, and then I tried to elaborate on some of the images and feelings that has swept over me as I stood in the midst of the Sidhe and the Stones—the Dancers and the Stones—in my living room.

"In addition to being a portal, a point of connection between worlds, the Stone Circle is also a Grail, a Cauldron in which stellar, solar, lunar, and planetary energies are mixed and blended with streams arising from life itself, from the deep spirit and sacredness underlying all. I can see potent "elixirs" of living spirit and energy being formed and distributed out into a web of connections across the land. The Circles are cauldrons of planetary alchemy.

"This is precisely the kind of alchemical Grail that each of us is, as well, so in an interesting manner the Circles replicate in stone what we do naturally in our own beings. The Circles represent the incarnational process that we embody. This exercise, I believe, is an affirmation of this.

"But there is another element here. I'm not sure I have this right in all the details, but the sense of it was strong in the message from my Sidhe contacts. In the past, the Sidhe have acted as Guardians of the Circles, and one of the things they have Guarded against is us. I think part of this Guardianship was for our protection—some of the energies invoked and gathered within these Circles may have been too powerful and thus potentially harmful for most incarnate humans who were deeply into matter and not prepared for the encounter.

"But part of it was to protect the energies themselves from us; there are Sidhe who do not fully trust us, or have not in the past, and with good reason. There was concern, if I understand this rightly, that the potency and nature of the energies invoked and held in the cauldron of the Circles could be misused and misapplied by human beings too deeply enmeshed in the limitations and perspectives of matter-based consciousness.

"What struck me in this contact as this exercise was passed on to me was that it represented a gift of trust. The Sidhe seemed to be saying that we are ready to wear this Mantle of Guardianship now because the world needs it; it needs us to do so. It cannot be contained in a stone circle here and there but must live in the lives of humans out in the world. It's time for the alchemical work of planetary healing and transformation to be taken beyond the realm of the Sidhe, beyond the confines of the Stone Circles of the past, and into the lives of human beings—our lives. A lineage is being shared with trust and hope.

"I cannot begin to articulate the feelings that come with this. What has made writing this exercise difficult for me has been the deep felt sense of being handed something—of all of us being handed something—very precious, perhaps even fragile, and easily distorted, and yet something also very strong and resilient and powerful. I have felt a weight of responsibility to get it right.

"It feels like an initiation to me into being one with the Sidhe, of sharing a mantle they have carried but doing so in a new way, in our human, incarnate way, within us as individuals who are also living Grails, living Circles."

I then presented the exercise as I had transcribed and interpreted it from the images that Mariel had shown me and from my own experience in the Presence of the Stones.

The Guardian Mantle Exercise

If you have a Card Deck of the Sidhe, keep it handy, but don't use it to begin with. Its use comes later in the exercise. If you don't have a Card Deck of the Sidhe, you can do all the steps perfectly well in your imagination.

- You begin by imagining yourself in front of an ancient stone circle, one that is rooted deep in the earth, the stones covered with moss and faint carvings. You can feel an energy radiating from it. Just as if you were going to enter someone's home, identify yourself and ask permission to step into the circle. Wait just a moment in silence, allowing yourself to be seen. The permission is granted.

- Step into the Circle. As you stand within it, surrounded by the presence of these ancient stones, it feels like you are in a great Cauldron held by Gaia. Into this Grail have poured over the centuries energies of consciousness and life brought into this world across the threshold of this Circle from sources distant and near: from stars, from the sun and moon, and from the deep fires of life within the heart of the earth. Here these forces are synthesized, blended into a wholeness and shared with the world.

- Although the Cauldron is empty as you stand in it, you can sense the power of holding within this place. You can feel the Grail in your own heart and life—your own powers of holding—resonating with it. Take a moment just to go deeply into the felt sense of this Circle Cauldron.

- Behind you and around you, felt but unseen, you sense the presence of the Guardians of this Circle and its Powers, Guardians of all it contains and all it connects. These are the Sidhe, and they welcome you into this place and their presence. Take a moment to go deeply into the felt sense of their ancient lineage of protecting and caring for the Life and Presence of Circles like this one.

- You are now asked, "Will you share this Guardianship with us? Will you take on the Mantle we have worn? Will you be part of the Lineage that guards the thresholds, opens the Cauldrons of loving spirit, and releases new Life into the World? Will you be an agent of wholeness in the world?" Take a moment to feel deeply and fully into what is being asked of you and what you think its implications may be for you personally in your life. How will you stand in this Lineage, wear this Mantle, and be a living Circle, Cauldron, or Grail in your world? When you feel ready, you can say "Yes" or "No."

- A "No" will not disconnect you from the Sidhe in any way nor be a mark against you. It is simply a statement that you feel this is not your path or that the timing is not right, or you don't fully understand what a Yes might mean or bring. A No is a statement of your sovereignty and is fully honored and blessed by the Sidhe. If you do say, "No," then receive the blessing of the unseen Guardians and step out of the Stone Circle. You can always reenter at another time that may be more appropriate.

- If you have said "No," take a moment to stand in your Sovereignty, and then go about your business in your everyday world. The exercise is ended.

- If you say "Yes," then take a moment of silence standing in the Circle among the Guardians, of whom you are now one. Be attentive in a calm way to anything that may occur or pass between the Sidhe and you.

- You have always been a Power of love and holding in the world and a threshold between the worlds. You have always been a Grail. Taking on the mantle of Guardianship which the Sidhe have offered only adds to what you already are, affirming it, anchoring it, giving it a new flavor and potential. Just what this means is what you will discover in your own unique way.

- At this point, the stones in the Circle begin to shimmer with Light. They dissolve and flow joyously and easily into your heart. Take a moment to feel the presence of the Circle shining within your being, your life, your heart. You ARE the Circle, the Portal, the Cauldron, the Grail. You have always been these things, but now you engage with them in a new way that will unfold in the days and months and years ahead.

• If you have the *Card Deck of the Sidhe*, now is the time to lay out a Stone Circle with the Howe in the middle. As you do so, see yourself externalizing the power of the Circle into your life and world. The Stone Circle has transmigrated from the Land to your Life. You are a Guardian of its power and presence within your life. *[If you do not have a Card Deck of the Sidhe, simply imagine Standing Stones flowing out from your heart to take shape around you.]* Take a moment to stand in the midst of the Circle of your own Life and feel what it means to you.

• Now, with gratefulness to the Sidhe, to your own Sacredness, to Gaia, and to the Sacredness within all things, bring this exercise to a close. Stand in your sovereignty for a moment, and then go about your everyday business as a Circle of Light in your world.

After presenting the exercise in the Forum, I added the following afterthoughts to sum up some of what I was feeling about it. I was concerned that people might see this exercise simply as a way to have an experience of the Sidhe when in fact it was focused more on us than on them.

"If Sidhe show up while you're doing this exercise, then you want to go with that experience. However, I wish to emphasize that the objective of this exercise isn't to contact the Sidhe; just the opposite. It's really to contact the soul and energy of your humanity while standing in a Sidhe-created field so that through you something can be transmitted from the Sidhe into the collective human field.

"The Stone Circle grounds their larger presence, even if only in your imaginations, and you ground the collective spirit of

Humanity, again even if only in your imaginations. So in effect, this exercise is a ritual in bringing the collective spirit of the Sidhe into contact with the collective spirit of Humanity through you so that something important can be exchanged and transmitted. Your task is to commune as deeply and fully as you can with your sacred humanness; you stand in the circle as a representative of humanity at this time in our history, and this is the focus you want to keep. The Sidhe can then see and connect to Humanity through your eyes, your mind, your thoughts, your feelings."

It was interesting the reactions. Not everyone in the Forum did the exercise, and of those who did, a few said "No" to the mantle when it came to it. In fact, when I first did the exercise, I also found I couldn't say "Yes" at that time and needed to say, "No", instead. In analyzing this later, I felt that to do my work as a point of contact between Mariel and the human world, I needed to maintain some inner distance and objectivity, and I was concerned if I said yes to the idea of this Mantle, this objectivity might be lost. This turned out not to be the case, and some months later, I did the exercise again and this time, it felt right and good to answer the question it asks in the affirmative.

Right from the start, individuals began having powerful and even life-changing experiences with this exercise, confirming for me that it did carry a lot of power. In fact, one woman did it and was instantly healed of a medical problem she'd been suffering for some time; she called me in tears barely able to talk she was so moved, to tell me about it. (As far as I know, no one else has had such a dramatic experience!)

This Guardian Mantle exercise truly began to take on a life of its own as people in the Forum began sharing it with others and I began to get requests also to share it with people and groups who had not known of the Forum. Eventually, the exercise and the story behind it was featured in an article in Quest, the journal of the Theosophical Society, at the Editor's request. In all of this, I felt the Sidhe working behind the scenes to promote this simple affirmation of taking on the power of being a living Grail, a living circle in whom different worlds connect and who can become an agent of wholeness in the world.

Some weeks later, Mariel returned and offered some final comments on the Guardian Mantle Exercise.

The Stone Circles, both in your world and in ours, are places of power. They are Cauldrons in which the forces of stars and sun, moon and earth, life and purpose, the One and the Many may meet, mingle and be alchemized into something new for all the worlds. As such, they stand on the land, and have done so for millennia, as sources of that power that creates wholeness. Part of our joy, part of our work is to serve the process and life of the Cauldron Circles and guard them and the connections they focus.

But each of you—each person—is such a Cauldron as well, a Grail as you call it. You are the living embodiment of what the Stone Circles do for the land and for spirit. We cannot be guardians of your inner processes, of your inner Circle; we do not carry that mantle. But you can be. You can wear the mantle of guarding and embodying the alchemical Circle, the inner Grail, that is your life.

What I wish to pass on to you is companionship with us in being a Guardian of this process, we of the Cauldrons, you of the Grails. In this we share a joint guardianship, a joint mantle, even though it manifests differently. What I invite you to do with this exercise is to step into your own awareness of yourself as a Circle, a Threshold, a Grail, to be in your individual life what we are for the Stone Circles.

In this way, this alchemical process isn't located in just those places on the land where the great Circles once stood or still stand; it's everywhere you are, for it's in you. Now is the time in your history—and ours—for you to recognize this and become the Circle of Living Wholeness that you can be. In taking up this mantle, you are guarding your own incarnational process, your own soul's living purpose in coming to earth millennia ago and creating a Circle in which each life is a standing stone, a presence where you have stood in your sovereignty. The lineage to which we call you is the lineage of Life itself in the power of its unfolding and its wholeness.

This is why we gave you what you call the Guardian exercise. It is only the tip of a larger process. If you understand the spirit and depths behind and within this exercise, you will begin to understand what we do, the mantle we carry. This is what we wish to share with you so it becomes your mantle as well. The form of the exercise is not critical but the spirit behind it is, and it is a spirit that you can share and elaborate in your own ways if you understand it.

For now, I leave you with this idea. The stone circle is a symbol of the portal that links the stars to earth; when you stand in it, you stand for the earth in its cosmic environment, mediators between stars and planet and midwives to the fullness of Gaia that emerges from this relationship. We are star people not because we come from the stars; you come from the stars as well. We are star people because we bring the stars to earth. But we can only bring them so far; there is a threshold we cannot cross, but you can, if you will dance the stars inward and outward with us. The Guardian exercise is an acceptance of being a star person in yourself. This is part of the mantle.

Until another time, blessings and joy!

CHAPTER SIX
An Experiment

After the Guardian Mantle exercise was given, it became obvious that my relationship with Mariel and with the Sidhe in general was going to be an ongoing phenomenon. If anything, I had a sense of a long-term project that she and her colleagues were developing, one—as she herself had said—that had "stages" in its unfoldment.

I felt that whatever this project might be, it would benefit from the attention and participation of a group. As my own involvement with the Sidhe had grown, I discovered that a number of my friends and colleagues, in addition to John Matthews and R. J. Stewart, also had contact with these beings. Some of them had worked with the Sidhe for years while others had begun having their own contact as a result of using the *Card Deck of the Sidhe*. It occurred to me that having some form of peer review or collaboration in which we could exchange information about our contacts and experiences would be of benefit to all of us. Anything that enhanced our knowledge of the Sidhe would help both parties to this evolving relationship.

As a consequence, in April of 2013, I organized a special online conference for individuals whom I knew who were actively working with the Sidhe in one way or another. I saw it as a gathering of "professional Sidhe-contactees" with the objective of comparing our "field notes" in order to broaden our understanding both of the Sidhe themselves and also of how to collaborate with them. While I knew many people who were interested in the Sidhe and would have eagerly joined such a gathering had they known about it, I limited participation to those who had a regular, active, working relationship of one kind or another. I invited John Matthews, but he regretfully let me know he simply did not have the time in his busy schedule to participate, and I expected the same was true for R.J.

As it turned out, this conference was successful and did give all of us more insights. Some of the messages I've already shared from Mariel about herself, her work and her people were given in response to questions asked in this conference which lasted on and off online for several months, alternating bursts of participation with long periods when no one had anything to share.

I mention this here because of an experiment that we conducted, and it's this experiment I wish to share.

In my work of fifty years with various beings from the subtle worlds, I was trained and accustomed to translating their communications into words that could be shared with others. It's not a perfect system, and inaccuracies and misinterpretations can occur, but by now, I have enough experience to keep these to a minimum or at least to be aware of when they might be likely to occur and let people know accordingly.

As I have said, contact with the Sidhe was different from contact with beings from the subtle worlds, but my work of taking the energy of such contacts with its raw meaning and impressions and translating them into words is basically the same. So I was accustomed to receiving what Mariel had to say and writing it out to share with others. Others in the group might have as good or better a contact with the Sidhe than I, but few had my particular training in turning the contact into words. We all recognized that this could be a problem if the group depended too much on my articulations, and at one point, Mariel herself addressed this issue:

I have said that as we approach your world and your consciousness, we become more "cloud-like" and less formed. This aids us in configuring with you and blending our minds with yours. But in so doing, we take on characteristics of your mental fields. So a conversation with me held by David will not be exactly the same as a conversation with me held by anyone else. There are our individual differences and yours as well which affect our communications together. No two people see things exactly alike, and this is true for the Sidhe as well.

This is why we do not wish you to rely only on one or two people for our communications. The contribution of different sensibilities on your part will result in a more well-rounded "mix" of perceptions and mind-qualities, allowing our nature and thoughts to unfold more fully in your midst. We try to speak with each of you in ways unique to the bond we form with your individual qualities of mind. Do not diminish what you can contribute in this regard by thinking that others have more facility in this process than you. David, for instance, is trained to articulate the nuances of the subtle worlds, but his mind gives them a particular spin—and there are things he does not and cannot see that another might perceive. We need you all, and we need you confident in your capacities to engage with us. Blessings!

With this in mind, we decided to conduct an experiment. One of the participants had asked me what the relationship of the Sidhe was to the Christ, assuming that I could ask Mariel. Instead, I put the question out to the group and asked everyone who wished to or could to ask this question through their own contacts. Then we could compare the answers, which would be posted simultaneously online.

We got four replies, which I reproduce below.

The first one is from Mariel.

More than for you who are embodied in matter's denser fabric, the Light is a known and present Quality for us. Sacredness is part of our world, experienced in many ways and though not necessarily in its full and supernal nature. We live in a luminous world within which joy is a constant presence if we wish it to be. There are those of us who have developed (or perhaps I should say have never lost) a deep and abiding capacity to take this joy and Light into themselves and act as Lightbearers to the rest of us. These individuals are not priests or ministers as you would understand those terms, nor are they exactly avatars. We are all avatars of the sacred, just as you are. They are those who have chosen to walk with higher Powers and make the results of their communion available to their brothers and sisters. We hold these individuals in high regard, perhaps as you would honor the Christ in your world, though we do not look upon them as exclusive embodiments of the Divine. And some of them have given great and needed service to our race, moving our evolution forward, though not by dying for us.

Because of this, we never needed, nor did we receive, a manifestation of sacredness comparable to your Christ. This great Soul's mission was to carry the Light and the Presence of Love into the deepest recesses of your material world, thereby affecting the vibrational structure of your world. In a way, the mission of this Being was set in motion by the very deep descent into matter which your race made—and ours did not. This descent had consequences for you, in addition to splitting us asunder, and the Christ came to redress these consequences. So in this regard, the Christ is a specifically human phenomenon. But though this being did not come for us, his presence affects us because it affects the world as whole on both sides of the divide between physical and non-physical existence. Remember that our world and our needs are different from your own. The redemption we need is different from your own, though in the largest sense, redemption could be understood simply as the restoration of wholeness and of the capacity to create and maintain it; in this largest sense, the redemption of both our worlds is fundamentally the same which would make any great Being who serves the restoration of wholeness on the planet an avatar for both our races. Nevertheless, the specific needs of your race and world and ours are different, so an avatar who serves you may not offer the same benefit to us and vice versa.

Also, you must differentiate between the Incarnation of a planetary soul with a mission of human redemption and a principle of sacredness itself that can take form and live amongst you. To repeat, we have the latter and did not need the former. But this is not because we are "more spiritual" than you. It is because of who and where you are in the planetary ecology and who and where we are.

However, there were those among us who helped with the Incarnation of Jesus and others who were attracted to it and to the Light and Love his life and ministry anchored into the deep substance of the Earth. There are those among us who could be called followers of the Nazarene, of the Incarnated Light, and some who continue to assist this Great One's mission. Certainly, none of us would oppose it.

Many of us are more aligned with the feminine side of the Sacred, and of these, there are those who respond to the Light of the Marys. The "Marian" line of energy and service is actually older than that which manifested through Jesus and extends back into the time when our races were still one. It is a line of energy of which I am a part. Indeed, there is a legend among us that the Mother of Jesus was of our lineage, that the blood of the

Sidhe ran in her veins so that Jesus became in his personage a reconciliation of our two peoples.

The Light and Love of Christ works for the wholeness of all, so in this sense it does bring our worlds together, and in our work, we seek a comparable objective. So we would see your Christ as our brother and co-worker. And as I say, there are those among our people who would seem Christ-like to you though they do not carry the mantle and the burden of planetary redemption and wholeness.

We recognize and honor the Christ in your lives, and to the extent Christ is a spark that lights the flame of your own sacredness, we are a breath to nurture that flame.

About two hours after receiving the above, while I was out for a walk, Mariel came back with a postscript:

There are those among us, very ancient even for our race, who remember the man Jesus and may even, if I am not mistaken, have interacted with him. The story I am told is that he was a man not unlike us in some ways, a man of joy and attunement to the world around him, particularly in his childhood and youth. Some of us, I am told, even acted as guardians of his well being. This is not surprising. I have already told you of the tradition among us that his mother Mary was of a Sidhe lineage herself, so Jesus would have had Sidhe blood within him if this tradition is correct—and I believe it is. But he was primarily of your race for this is what his mission demanded. He was a crossroads in whom many "roads" of consciousness and life met and were brought into connection and wholeness, for wholeness is the essence of redemption, as I have said.

We are beings of joy, and joy for us is much, much more than an emotion. It is for us akin to sunshine for you, a force that energizes, organizes, and nourishes life. We live in the Light of the Sun of Joy. This is what Jesus embodied. To use your own phrasing, he was and is the Son of Joy and brought this Light into your world. This is very Sidhe-like, but he did so not as one of us but as one of you. He is a Light of Human Joy. But Joy is Joy, whatever its source, and wherever its Light is present can be home to us.

Ian Rees is a psychotherapist living in Glastonbury, England. Yearly, his practice also takes him to Jerusalem where he does group work group work with therapists and social workers on the processes of personal and collective healing. As I discovered, Ian has been in contact with the Sidhe for many years and has received help from them in his psychotherapeutic work. This was the response that he received (he added his own comments as well which I have put into italics or into parenthesis).

We have our own relationship to the being you call the Christ which we experience as a radiant living field of emergence which produces a densification of experience for us and multiplies the possibilities of the expression of our being. The group of the Sidhe that I am part of co-operate with this being and are similarly drawn to working with incarnate human beings to enable the next step for both human and Sidhe. I call myself Melusine when I communicate with you, not just because I am fond of making jokes about being the dragon lady (*she is fond of appearing in a stylised Chinese half-dragon, half-woman form as a way of getting away from Tolkienesque images of the Sidhe*) but because the legends of Melusine point to the work of my group.

[In essence, Melusine's story is of a Sidhe woman from Avalon who guards a fountain in the midst of a deep forest, and of a human man who accompanies his Lord on a boar hunt into the forest. They are attacked by a wild boar, and the young man kills both the old boar and the old lord. He carries the bodies of his lord and the boar to the fountain and agrees to marry the lady of the fountain. As a result, he is raised to lordship, is given land, and she builds the castle of Lusignan from out of the deep places of the consecrated land. They live together happily while he keeps a promise that he will allow her to be secluded each seventh day when she becomes half-dragon, half-woman and immerses herself in a deep tub. Eventually, he breaks his promise, and she returns to her own land but watches over her children, becoming associated eventually with the Crusader Kingdom of Jerusalem.]

This is an ancient human myth about the emergence of the new from the old and the marriage of the Sidhe and the human. It is also a story of loss and renewal, and the old myth has much in it that can teach you of the work of my group and the need for humans and Sidhe to embrace each other. It is linked with the consecration of the land and the building of an inner structure which enables life to flow and bring life and fertility to all. The story leads us to Jerusalem and the work of the man you call Jesus who was for us a great nexus and point of union whose light shone in both worlds and who was with us even as he was with you. He was one who had made the marriage and had built the temple, so was able to exercise a rare priesthood. There are some beings among our people who are likewise anointed in this way who stand in white stillness and manifest the golden light of emergence; the marriage of opposites that appears in this place means the human must embrace our fluid immortality while the Sidhe must embrace death and mortality.

The work of Jesus earthed and made visible the marriage; it quickened the life of all. A key aspect of his work, for us, was the tearing down of the Temple and the creation of what he called the temple of his body and the creation of the Graal cup which holds his potentised blood. This blood is the blood of the union of human and Sidhe that transmits the power of the living Christ or the energy of anointing and multiplication of the possibilities of emergence transmitted through the cup of his body.. This for us is the centre of his work and also that of Mary, who brings to us the energies of birth and forms the container; she is the mother who nourishes the flame and weaves it in and out of being. Mary is to us both human woman and vast ancient being whose deep stillness nurtures the flame of being. Mary is the cup containing the united blood and the Christ flame that manifests. Communion with her enables the manifestation of the Graal within you.

The image you have included of human and fairy holding the lance which pierces Christ next to the tower of alchemy graphically shows the work. It is the mixing of starblood and the ironblood of earth, which is one way of describing this *(alchemical)* marriage. This has reference to the actual blood cells of the body as well as many other levels: at its simplest, it is no more than

the acknowledgement of relationship with the Sidhe and all else
will come of that.

Ian included with his message the following picture, which he said
his contact, Melusine, insisted on being shared. He said it's a sixteenth
century woodcut titled "The Composition of the Elixir", dated to 1582.
It shows the Faery Melusine as a crowned woman with a reptilian tail.
She and an unclothed woman identified as Eve together pierce the breast
of Christ, allowing red and white blood—the mingled and unified blood
of human and Sidhe, of the earth and the stars—to flow to the ground.
Next to the figures is the symbol of an alchemical castle representing the
forces that create wholeness out of separate elements. So here are the
invisible forces of the Sidhe and the spirit realms working with the human
elements of the earth represented by Eve to release the potentised blood
of Christ into the world to create healing and wholeness.

Susan Stanton Rotman lives on the East Coast of the United States.
At one time a successful attorney, she now works as an intuitive counselor
drawing on her life-long talents for working with the subtle worlds.
She, too, has been in contact with the Sidhe for many years; in fact, her
granddaughter calls her "Grandma Sidhe" in part due to her red hair.
She sent the following as a result of her contact with the Sidhe about this

question of their relationship to the Christ.

I have a spectacular feeling sense and image of the Christ: I see an intensely brilliant light, almost like a star if you were up close to it—a center of intense white and yellow light, radiating out. It is not spherical, but more elongated than that, a kind of diamond or elongated oval shape, hard to tell—because of its brilliance it is hard to find defining edges. This is a source, alive and generating, radiant. It has the feel of both a heart and mind, the soul of oneness. It has consciousness, and it expands continuously, reaching out with innumerable rays and penumbras and showers of this radiant, conscious source light. It has some kind of a pulse or a rhythmic cycle to it, not quite a heart beat but reminiscent of that, or perhaps a beacon cycling, but something unique with a quality of contracting and expanding regularly. It is palpably sharing and conveying an ineffable sense of what I can only identify as pure love. It is embracing and engagement with it gives a sense of complete well being.

The Sidhe have great respect for this, it is as if they bow before this. They recognize this as life force and source and much more. The Sidhe, while usually appearing and feeling to me as quite tall, look small before the Christ. This is not a statement of size or importance, but rather a reference point to help convey how vast the Christ consciousness is.

The Sidhe are very familiar with the Christ, although they do not identify it or experience it in the conventional terms that religions identify as Jesus. Jesus is also small compared to the vastness of the Christ, even while he was very large in his incarnation here.

The Sidhe recognize the Christ as an origin or source of the generative light of creation. They identify with this light not only because of their own light, which is an extension in some degree from this source, but also because they vibrate, or resonate, at a refined "speed" or level which is attracted to the vibrational level of the Christ, as if the Christ is a tuning fork of sorts which the Sidhe are able to set themselves to.

Humans are also aware of the vibrational tone or feel of the Christ, but without the level of attunement of the Sidhe. Humans are also an extension from the Christ source, just as the Sidhe are, but in very different frequency ranges. This is not to say the Sidhe are better, but only that their form allows attunement more easily, it is really a matter of vibration and frequencies. Human form is more dense and cannot convert or step down the very intense refined frequencies of the Christ, and the Sidhe are less dense and therefore somewhat better able to attune their frequencies to the Christ vibration. This is not to say that humans cannot, but only that their wiring makes it more tedious to do so.

Because of these differences, the Sidhe may be able to serve as step down adapters for us in attuning to the Christ field. This seems to me to be about physics and frequencies and sound and light and the movement of these forces.

There is something here about the Sidhe mediating these forces. They are able, and willing, to serve as relays in some way—bringers of the light.

Adrienne McDunn is one of the people most responsible for starting this whole cycle of events with the Sidhe. She has had her own contact with these "cousins" for some time, and it was also to her that they expressed their desire that a card deck be created. As I related in the Introduction, this desire, communicated to Jeremy Berg, ultimately led to Mariel's contact with me and the creation of the Sidhe Deck. More than just stimulating the project in the first place, Adrienne was able to fund it as well. Card decks are expensive to produce; the project might have stopped had her generosity not provided the means that enabled Jeremy to undertake the costs of the production.

When she made contact to answer this question of the relationship of the Sidhe to the Christ, it was not the former but the latter who responded.

The Avatar speaks:

The Sidhe and Humans are ancestors of each other.

There used to be a direct relationship between the two. Or I should say more aligned relationship. The original People experienced the incarnational flow most profoundly. Attuned to this essence, they were not attached to that which manifested as a result of their engagement. But their focus, and ear as it were, was on the attunement.

After some time some did turn their attention to that which was manifesting and desired to engage it more fully. After a while, as is the way of such things, the desire created a reality.

For a long time the two groups worked together as aspects of creation were exchanged freely. One group focused on the sacred attunement, the other focused on engagement with creation. Over time however, the groups found it harder to maintain a connection and it was even difficult to exist in one another's territory.

After a while exchange among the peoples became more difficult. They lost their alignment and ceased to understand that they are two aspects of one creation. They began to diverge as a people. Not all forgot but their capacities to connect increased in difficulty as the peoples moved away from one another in physical creation.

I came to Earth to directly seed the cosmic principle of Incarnation in this Realm. This power, initially given to the People, became distorted as the Peoples created distance between them. And, thus the man Jesus became the incarnation of this power or quality. This the Sidhe could not do, even if they had a will to do it, for their alignment with Humanity had weakened. The direct seeding gave to this Realm capacity for sacred attunement as well as capacity for sacred creation.

As Humanity develops capacities to join, align, and embody this Incarnational Impulse they will right their relationship with the Source of Creation. They can also align with the Sidhe if they will it. It is desirable but not necessary. Humanity will work with the Incarnational force one way if they do not reconnect with the Sidhe and another way if they do. The latter will be more difficult for both groups.

The Incarnational Host grows stronger in Humanity, not perhaps in numbers, but in the capacities of the few to hold it and work with it. This would be a good time, in this development, for Humanity to connect with the Sidhe to align efforts. As Humanity discovers its capacity for co creation this will enable the connection and ability to work with the Sidhe. But even if Humanity does not do this the Sidhe will be affected by the efforts of Humanity to engage the Incarnational Impulse. They will benefit although they have no hand in the results. They do I think prefer to initiate direction but that is another matter.

The relationship of the Sidhe to the Christ remains intact although having lost direct contact with aspects of their sacred outflow they no longer have as much influence over it or the Earth Realm. Or it becomes increasingly harder for them to exert an influence.

Their relationship with the Jesus of the Christ is that of opportunity. It remains to be seen if they will avail themselves of this opportunity.

As an experiment among this group of people working with the Sidhe, I felt the results were interesting and informative. Here are four different responses to one question, and it's fascinating to see both the similarities and the differences. As Mariel said, different contacts working through different minds will produce unique results. Yet, in spite of the differences, there is still a consistent, coherent picture that underlies and emerges from these four responses.

Sometime later, reviewing these results, I asked Mariel if she had further thoughts about how this experiment went.

You should not be surprised. Have I not said that we are a people as diverse in our ways as you and that we do not all speak with one voice. I do not speak for all the Sidhe, only for those of my "faction", as you term it, who have undertaken this project with you. But consider, if you asked about the Christ, would you not get a different picture from one of his followers than you would from a follower of the Buddha or one who participates in Islam? Even among Christians, would you not find differences? What would be more surprising is if all said the same thing.

However, as you can see, there are common threads weaving through the responses from me and others of my kind. The Christ is important to us, though not always in the same way as he is for you and not always in the same way between us. We celebrate all the great Lightbringers among your people and ours. Some, like Buddha, are well known to you, but some are lost to your history because they lived their lives and did their work quietly out of sight, unknown Standing Stones in the great circle of planetary life.

The incarnation of the Christ brought to you, as incarnate humans, insights and connections with the Sacred that are not open to us or at least not as easily. We have our own awareness of the One Light, of the Sacred, but you have an awareness of that Light within matter, and more, you have awareness of that Light within sacrifice. You can know the Sacred in ways we do not because of this, and it is one of the things we seek to learn from you even as we share with you the lightness and joy of our inner being.

This latter idea, that we know an aspect of Sacredness that the Sidhe do not but which they wish to know, is a powerful one. It defines part of the relationship and potential between us and what the two "cousins" can offer each other. Nor was this the last time this subject arose. It came up again as a result of the class which Mariel, Jeremy and I taught together.

This class is the subject of Part II.

PART II

THE CLASS

INTRODUCTION

In December and January, I plan out the main classes I'm going to teach for the following year so that they can go up on the calendar on the Lorian website in plenty of time for people to sign up. As 2013 gave way to 2014, however, something new and unexpected was added. The experience with the online Sidhe conference site plus the spread of the Guardian Mantle exercise seemed to give new momentum to Mariel and her companions. So one day, Mariel came to ask if I would join with Jeremy in sponsoring an actual online class on the Sidhe.

At first I had reservations. Jeremy had done workshops on the Sidhe using the *Card Deck of the Sidhe* as a teaching aid, but I never had. It was outside my usual area of knowledge and skill. What, exactly, would a class on the Sidhe consist of? What would we do? "That's what we'll find out," Mariel said in true Sidhe fashion. "It will unfold in the moment. It will be as much of an experiment for us as it will be for you."

I contacted Jeremy, and we talked about it. I shared with him that I could feel Mariel's interest, in doing this class; there even was a sense of pressure to do so, but it was the pressure of listening to a finely-tuned automobile engine rev up before a race and knowing that it was ready to go. Jeremy was all for going ahead, and the more I thought about it, the more I knew as well it was something we needed to do.

So *An Exploration into the Sidhe* was put on the Lorian class list for April of 2014 as a six-week online class. As the time approached for it to begin, neither Jeremy nor I had any more idea of what was going to happen or what we were going to do than we had had when we agreed to do the class. Ah, Improvisation! Thy name is Sidhe!

However, though I felt no specifics coming from Mariel's side of things, I did feel what I can only describe as a "sphere of energy" building up to support the class. It was like fuel being stockpiled to run the race car whose engine was revving up. I have often had this experience when working with subtle beings, and it gave me confidence that when the time came, the energy would be there to make something happen. Beyond that, I didn't need to know. I may be part-Sidhe myself for I love improvisation and allowing things to unfold in the moment. It's how I run most of my classes anyway.

As it turned out, I need not have been concerned. The class turned out to be full and rich. The participants were a wonderful mix of individuals who were encountering the idea of the Sidhe for the first time and others who were old hands at it, including some who had taken part in the online Sidhe conference and had their own ongoing contact with our invisible cousins. As the class unfolded, Mariel came through in spades, offering one communication after another.

It is these communications that make up the bulk of Part II of this book.

One interesting element was that a certain amount of energy had been shaped and allotted to this class to support Mariel in connecting and communicating with us. This became more and more clear to me as we went along, because I could feel this "sphere of energy" or fuel being used and I could feel it running out. It was as if she had received a certain amount of "funding" for this project from her end, and each time she contacted us or supported the very evident and powerful field of supportive energy that everyone in the class felt at one time or another, a bit of this funding was spent. It was not "personal money", that is to say, it wasn't Mariel's personal energy or that of any other particular Sidhe. It was "project money", a collective field of energy that was tailored to do a specific task, and when it was gone at the end of six weeks, it was gone. Frankly, I'd never experienced anything quite like it.

There were some who wished the class could have gone on longer, but it was not possible. The allocated energy had been used, and Mariel needed to withdraw to recharge her own batteries. For that matter, mine needed some recharging as well, for any contact with non-physical beings and forces, whether from the subtle worlds or from the Sidhe, is work and takes both physical and mental energy.

As an experiment to create and hold a powerful field of contact and collaboration between the Sidhe and a number of humans all working together, I think it was successful. It certainly felt that way at the end. Will we do it again? I have no idea, but one thing I've learned with the Sidhe over the past three years: never say never.

THE SIDHE AND HUMANITY:
A Modest History

[I began the class by writing an article on the history of the relationship between the Sidhe and Humanity. I've decided to add it here because even though it repeats some of the information already found in Part I, it puts it altogether in a single document which you may find useful. Feel free to skip over this and go right to the communications from Mariel, if you wish.]

The Sidhe (pronounced shee) are a race of diverse beings who live in one of the realms invisible to us that make up the larger ecology of the Earth. My understanding is that they are not subtle beings, i.e. spirits or non-physical entities. Their world exists on a "wavelength" of the physical dimension, even though they obviously are not part of the physical wavelength or environment where we live. They are incarnated individuals who are very long-lived, though not immortal, and who have their own unique relationship to what I call the Subtle Worlds. Like us with our various races and ethnicities, they come in different "flavors" or types, differentiations that are enhanced by the fact that their bodies are capable of shape-shifting to a greater or lesser degree.

As we go on in the class, I'll be posting communications from my primary Sidhe contact, a woman I've named Mariel, who from time to time has commented on the history of her people and their relationship to humanity. What I want to do here is to summarize my best understanding of this history as I've gleaned it from the Sidhe contacts I or Jeremy have had and that others have had.

A theme found in many Sidhe contacts is that they are related to humanity—R.J. Stewart calls them our "cousins"—and that, as Mariel has said, we once shared a common ancestor. However, at various times in our history, we have moved apart, sometimes amicably and sometimes not, ultimately forming two separate peoples. In so doing, something that had been whole in both of us was sundered and is in need of repair and reconciliation. It's this reconciliation and the discovery of this ancient wholeness that is a thread running through most of Mariel's communications and at times through the communications that others have received.

The following history is my best attempt at telling this story, based on conversations with my own subtle colleagues, friends such as John

Matthews, and with Mariel herself. I'm quite sure it's incomplete, and I'm aware that there are many details left out. But hopefully, it will give at least an overview of what we're dealing with.

Just as the Earth floats through space as a physical sphere, so it exists in a vast cosmic subtle universe in which it is a distinct field of life and consciousness. It possesses a "world soul" holding within its purview countless trillions of other evolving lives who call this planet home. While the World Soul is in constant communion and communication with the cosmic spiritual environment, there are times when a particular "wave" of interaction takes place. At such times, the Earth may receive an influx of new consciousnesses, as well as having waves that move on, having gained what they needed or could receive from this particular planetary environment. Remember, we're not talking about anything physical here. These transactions and comings and goings are at an energetic level and represent the movement of souls, not people in space ships!

One of the waves that came to Earth millions of years ago contained the seeds of what are now both the Sidhe and humanity. At that time, they formed a unified field of consciousness, what I think of as a "cosmic humanity." We need to think of this "wave" as arriving over a period of millions of years, coming in stages much as a tide moves up the beach in stages; each stage laid down a pattern that supported the emergence of the next stage.

As I understand it, the biosphere was only just forming at this time. All of the incarnational activity of this early cosmic humanity took place in the subtle realms of the planet. It was during this period that what we would recognize as the human soul began to take form as cosmic humanity progressively engaged with the energies and substance of the World Soul.

Again, as I understand it, none of the beings that came in those first waves remains on Earth today. They moved on and were replaced by what we might think of as "descendents" or at any rate by those who carried on the process and built on what the previous stage had accomplished. Think of the Greek myths of the Earth and Sky (Gaia and Uranus) mating to give birth to the Titans who in turn were replaced by the Olympians (such as Zeus, Apollo, Athena, and so on) who then gave way to humanity. Many cultures around the world have similar myths of successive generations of gods that finally end with the arrival of humanity as we know it today.

As time went on, the incarnational process went deeper into the planetary subtle fields moving eventually into the Incarnate Realms such as the realms of thought, feeling, and eventually the etheric. By this time, the wave of cosmic humanity that was most active were the progenitors of humanity as we now know it, souls that stood on the edge of full incarnation into physical form. This wave contained what Mariel, my Sidhe contact, has called our "common ancestor".

However, even then, there was a pulling apart. There were those who sought the experience of deeper incarnation into matter, those who felt it best to remain in the more subtle dimensions, those who were willing to enter etheric substance but no further, and so on. Some of this pulling apart had purpose; it was felt important that humanity as a whole have part of its collective field close to the Earth and the physical plane and part closer to the realm of Souls, providing a full spectrum of connection and expression.

But some of this pulling apart by some members of the common human energy field seems to have been in resistance to moving deeper into more dense and constricted conditions of physical incarnation. And it was here that the split between Sidhe and Humanity began to take place. Many Sidhe took the plunge, so to speak, and became human, forming an incarnational partnership with the evolving primates that resulted in what we would recognize as human consciousness being formed. Some Sidhe took the plunge but held onto their Sidhe form, becoming a related but distinct species

According to Mariel, many of the Sidhe who did not wish to fully enter the physical world went so far as to create a "pocket dimension" of their own out of astral and etheric matter, a part of the world that was incarnate but not fully, a world in-between the physical and the non-physical that was strongly shaped by the imagination of the Sidhe. Some of the Sidhe who went more fully into physical incarnation later retreated into this *Sidhe-verse* when they felt pressured by the expanding population of incarnate human beings.

Apparently for a long time relationships between these two evolving species that had at one time been one united field of life were good. There were matings between them and a mixing of bloodlines, and there were gatherings that took place at certain times of the year, often around or related to portals anchored in the earth through a geomantic art that eventually began using standing stones. But in time, relationships became strained, then severed, and the two "cousins" moved farther apart, especially as humanity gradually lost the capacity to easily sense the subtle worlds and technology began to appear to take the place of inner powers that became dormant.

Basically, then, the Sidhe are a people like ourselves pursuing their own course of evolution and possessing their own civilization. But as Mariel has said, they inadvertently boxed themselves in to an evolutionary cul-de-sac since the world they inhabit is of their own shaping and imagining. It reflects them back to themselves in a way that does not allow ease of movement beyond what is familiar.

So they need what we can offer from our experience with evolution and the ability to innovate and change, and we need what they offer in their connection to the world and to the forces of wholeness.

The Sidhe are often associated and even identified with nature spirits, but they are not such beings. They have close connections with nature spirits—closer than we do now—and I think help to shape and bring certain kinds of nature beings ("lesser faeries") into existence. But they are not nature spirits or devas themselves, any more than we are. Still, their closeness to the realms of nature and even more importantly, to the formative powers of the earth and of human consciousness hold a promise of wholeness for us.

Why bother with the Sidhe? Contact with the Sidhe opens up new ways of thinking about the challenges that humanity is facing and the help we can receive. Contact with the Sidhe can be exciting for its own sake, but the deeper purpose behind reconciliation is to break through the bubble that is forming around humanity due to the increasingly self-referential and human-centric attitudes and behaviors that characterize industrial and technological society. In this sense, the Sidhe become exemplars for us, though not with the purpose of surrounding us with glamour or turning us away from our humanity. Rather they would help us discover a larger, fuller humanity that can embrace both them and us and in the process, create a new and helpful collaborative relationship. We need to break out of the human-centric bubble but not in a way that damages our humanity. Paradoxically, the Sidhe, by mirroring what a Gaian humanity might be like, can help us accomplish this.

Why bother with the Sidhe? Because they are our kin and because in discovering the mystery of their being, we may better discover the mystery and wonder of our own.

MARIEL'S CLASS MESSAGES
APRIL, 2014

As soon as the class started, Mariel offered her first message. She followed this up slowly. For the first couple of weeks, I mainly posted many of the messages I've already shared with you in Part I. But as the momentum and energy grew in the class, she began to come more and more frequently, both answering questions and offering her own insights. By the end, she was offering something nearly every day.

The following messages are presented in the chronological order in which they were given in the class. I have given each of them a title for convenience, indicating the main theme of the message.

WELCOME TO THE CLASS

Greetings! We are called together into an experiment in contact and collaboration between your realm and mine, your people and mine. We have hopes for this time together, but we do not know what will be the outcome. Still, unless a seed is planted, no fruit will appear. This class is such a seed.

It is true that the impetus for doing this class at this time comes from us. It is part of our effort at building new bridges between us. As such, it continues in the same vein as the effort that brought forth the cards that you use in our name. These cards, unlike others with which you are familiar, are not intended primarily for divination or the satisfying of questions. They should be understood as a portal through which our mutual life energies and consciousnesses may meet and interact. They are designed to bring into a mobile form the presence of the stone circles that have been portals for us for millennia. In this sense, they are not unlike one of your cell phones, a miniaturization of a structure of contact.

Your purpose in participating in this gathering may be to learn about us, we whom you call the Sidhe. You may have many reasons for this, and some of these reasons may be cloaked in glamours of one kind or another that we will need to disperse. Whatever brings you here at this time, you are welcome and you have our gratitude and blessing.

Our purpose is not to focus upon ourselves, though I know you are curious. We are interested in two things. The first is to use the mobile portal to explore connections between your realm and our own; in this we are seeking to build what you might call a force field that will unite, bless and inform all card decks wherever they are used. Working with this project together through the medium of the cards will enhance this. The second reason is our desire for you to see and know yourselves in new ways. This time on earth is calling for the appearance of a new expression of humanity, one that can draw on ancient threads of connection with the planet. While we are not asking you to become like us, we do see that a "Sidhe-like" aspect of your own being—held in you since we both were part of a common ancestor—is needed to arise. We wish to nourish this.

In all honesty, we are not entirely clear how to do this, for in many ways you are a mystery to us now much as we are a mystery to you. We hope in our gathering to throw light to illumine these mysteries. More importantly, perhaps, you are also a mystery to yourselves, and it's this mystery we would help you penetrate and unfold. What collaboration may look like between you and us is still evolving. There are those of our kind who do not support this effort or feel it is futile, much as many of your people see us as wisps of imagination of no significance to the world of matter. So there are obstacles before both of us.

But it's through occasions such as this one when we come together in a singleness of purpose to learn of our mutual natures and of the possibilities of cooperation that these obstacles may be overcome and the mysteries before us be resolved. We will not arrive at our destination all at once, but through this class and its exploration, we are taking a vital step towards it…and perhaps more steps than one. Blessings!

MARIEL'S "FACTION"—THE "STAR-WEAVERS"

Blessings!
We are much gratified with the class you are doing, gratified that you are doing it, gratified with the spirit and enthusiasm that

all participating are bringing to the enterprise. We are seeking to align with each of you through the energy of the class as a whole. It is an experiment for us as well as for you, and we shall see what unfolds.

I am aware there are questions about our mutual history and, as always, about our nature. After all, friends and partners want to know about each other.

In tracing the history of a people, the least effective way is with a straight line. It simplifies events and provides a narrative, but it leaves much out. For instance, in your own story, there was a time when your world contained more than one type of humanity. Your branch succeeded, the others did not, but they left their mark upon you and within you.

The same is true for us. The Sidhe are not a homogeneous people, any more than you are, nor have we ever been. Indeed, variation is more the rule for us than for you because of the malleability of our forms. You use technology to successfully occupy many environmental niches in your world, but we use the creative power of mind and what you might call "magic" to do the same thing in our world.

Just as your scientists have speculated on altering the human genome to create new forms of humans adapted to environments where normal humans could not thrive or even survive, so we have done this among ourselves, creating different forms of Sidhe to adapt to different conditions and realms within the earth. And we have cooperated and participated with the great Devas of nature to fashion forms that bear our imprint but are part of the realms of the nature spirits more than a part of our world. This has given rise in part to what you call the Faerie world. While some Faery are indeed Sidhe in native or in altered forms, others are hybrids born of our influence and creativity in partnership with the Soul of the World and her Devic handmaidens. Further, just as nature spirits may mimic and adopt forms and behavior from the human world, so do they at times mimic and adapt forms from our world.

It is also true that just as there have been waves of humanity that preceded your own, there have been waves of Sidhe preceding us, some of whom are still present among us. And at various times, branches of the Sidhe have sprung off and moved away from the main trunk, so to speak, particularly during the times when we and humanity were separating.

So there is much variation among us, which is as it should be, but it means when you think of us, you should not think of a single, unified people. We are all Sidhe but we are not all the same, just as you are all humanity but you are not all the same.

There are Sidhe who delight in shapeshifting and are adept at it. They can wear many faces and enjoy doing so. Not all of us participate in this. I, for instance, am not of the shapeshifting race, though I am capable of doing so. For ones such as myself, continuity and stability of form is important. With shapeshifting comes adaptability but also a loss of power and focus, both of which are regained when the form is allowed to settle and remain stable.

The faction I represent is fairly new among the Sidhe and comes forward in direct response to the changes taking place in the subtle bodies of the planet. We are keyed to the impulses of the future less than of the past, which is one reason we have not wished you to see us through the thought-forms of the older races and appearances of our Sidhe forebears. We are not, as I have said, part of a medieval kingdom, though we have resonance with those who are.

The Sidhe have always been people of the stars, just as you once were and still are in your depths. We remember our stellar and cosmic heritage more than you do yours, and even those Sidhe who most remove themselves from the world or who delight in the stylized forms of kingdom and court, or those who have gone deeply into the elemental and nature worlds, remember their connection to the stars and to the stellar populations that were our source before this world became our home. But some of us have cultivated this contact more directly and continuously, largely in preparation for the time the world is now entering when new waves of stellar energies are being absorbed by the planetary soul.

So my "faction", if I may term it such, is made up of those who are the singers of star songs and the weavers of stellar energies into the fabric of planetary space and time. We are as much a part of this world as you are—we are not cosmic visitors—but we hold our form stable and steady so we can receive and carry into the world the stellar energies that now bathe our planet. It is these energies we would share with you and in so doing, help you awaken in proper fashion your own stellar natures.

Stones have long been used to anchor the star-forces into the earth, making them available to the living world. The Stone Circle is not just a portal to our realm, a connection with us, but also an organ of respiration that connects the life breath of the stars with the lungs and body of the earth. This is shown in the image of the Howe that we first presented to Jeremy, that of the stars within the earth.

Breathe with us the life breath of the stars and bring a new vitality and spirit into your world.

Blessings!

THE STAR PRIESTESS

Greetings!

In my role amongst my people, I am a priestess of the stars. This sounds glamorous and exotic to human ear, but it is a particular role, one that enables me to cross the threshold between us and communicate with you. It is the star energy within humanity that I can touch and that forms a link between us.

I say this to explain my nature to you and the limitations that I experience, as well as to clarify our objectives in reaching out to you. My role is that of a mediator. I both walk upon and caretake the bridges that link my people to the stars. I am not a priestess in a religious sense such as you might understand. I am responsible for the ease and clarity of flow of stellar qualities of life into our world and now, if possible with human help, into your world.

When I speak of the stars, I mean much more than the points of light you see in the nighttime sky, the burning spheres of light and heat. The cosmos is alive with multitudes of beings and fields of consciousness. Stars are such fields of life and energy, most of them great beings. The earth is fostered and mentored by certain of them who are the sources from which many of the spiritual streams of consciousness came that ultimately became lifeforms upon the earth, including our own, yours and mine. The links with these ancient sources are still there, and my job is to cultivate and sustain them.

It is this work that brings me into contact with you, for humanity is under the care of certain of these star fields. You are at a point in your development in which awareness of these links is possible in ways different from what you have had in the past. It is also true that the subtle structure of the world is changing to accommodate a greater flow of influence and energy from these stellar sources. We are part of this change, as are you. It is our wish to collaborate with you in facilitating it.

I tell you this so that you may appreciate my "specialization". I am not an historian of our people, but there are those among us, the elders and the holders and singers of the tales of our lineages, who are. When you have questions about the past, it is to them that I must look and they determine what is proper for me to share. For our task—my task—isn't to satisfy your curiosity, wonderful as that might be, nor is it even to build the bridges between you, important as this is as well. My task is to help you discover and unfold your own link with the stars so that you may mediate their presence in your lives just as I do. My task is to enable you to stand as portals in your world, to the extent that you are able. My task is to help you discover the Stone Circle within you, the Circle that you are as an organic, physical being, and to link your circle with the stellar sources I serve and with Gaia as well. I work with you along the axis between the Gate of Stars and the Gate of Earth so that you can stand and work along the threshold between the Gate of Dawn and the Gate of Twilight. [Here Mariel is making reference to four of the cards in the *Card Deck of the Sidhe* and the vertical and horizontal cross they form together.]

My work is to pass on to you the mantle of being mediators of the stars, the mantle I wear as well. You will carry it differently than I do, and you will each carry it uniquely in yourself, differently from any other. Yet this mantle will link us together in ways that will unfold with discovery for all of us.

94

THE ORIGINS OF FAERIE

I am aware of your questions, though, for David passes them on to me, and I read them in the field we all create together. So let me share with you what I understand, what has been passed to me by those more elder and knowledgeable than I in this area.

The key to understanding lies in the dual nature of the human being, a duality we do not completely share with you though we have echoes of it in our nature, too.

Part of you has come to the world through the Gate of Stars. Part of you has arisen from the world through the Gate of Earth. In ancient times, these streams merged and produced humanity as you are today. Before the splitting of our peoples, we took part in some of this merging—we were a common people then—so we share some of this earthly heritage with you. But the most powerful merging occurred after we split as you fully entered into the physical realm and the realm of nature.

I have said that our split, which was progressive and occurred over a long period of time, not all at once, was due to a reluctance on our part to fully enter into matter. This is true, but it is not the full picture. There were other factors at work. Among these factors was the origin of what you might now call the realm of Faerie.

The origin of the Faerie realms is partly rooted in the physical history of your race. All species of life have their subtle companions, spirits of nature that attend to their development. One class of such spirits was tasked with developing a physical species capable of joining with human souls in order to bring forth physical humanity. In time several candidates came forward, evolving out of primate beginnings. Different types of human beings were tried out, so to speak, until your ancestral species proved most suitable and became fully imbued with the powers of mind and individuality that were the gifts of the incarnating human souls.

In this process, there arose beings who occupied a new niche within the planetary ecology on both the physical and subtle side. These different early human types were no longer part of the animal kingdom but they were not fully enabled or endowed by spirit to be the new human species. They occupied a middle ground, a liminal space filled with potential. Their souls or animating spirits were drawn directly from the sphere of nature spirits who had shepherded them into existence, so in a sense they were incarnations of these subtle beings who were themselves highly evolved for their kind. Further, they possessed the magic of their kind, a magic born of the inner realms and of their nature. We think of them as the Children of Gaia, just as you and we are Children of the Stars.

One of the objections raised by those of the Sidhe who did not wish to fully enter incarnation was a concern that a blend of our magical energy with that of these nature beings in physical incarnation would prove volatile. There were those of us who simply did not wish to go that deeply into matter or to take up the challenge of a material body, but there were those as well who feared what the combination of star magic and earth magic might produce.

[Note—I'm choosing the word "magic" here to translate what Mariel was showing me because I don't know any other word that quite fits, knowing full well that "magic", because of the glamour and misconceptions around it, doesn't quite fit either. Magic here isn't a power to hurl fireballs or work miracles but something more like an innate creative and shaping force—almost a kind of magnetism or electricity—unique to a species or to a particular kind of consciousness. "Star magic" and "earth magic" are my terms, not Mariel's, to suggest a differentiation here between what was being brought into the world by the Sidhe/Human soul ancestors and what was already here and innate to Gaia.—David]

So, you see, there were different reasons why the decision to enter into materiality and physical incarnation was not universally agreed to. But during this liminal period when the deep linking of star souls with earth body and earth life was happening, different forms of humanity emerged and with them new, allied forms of subtle beings, born of the fields of magic that were being generated. It was a powerful and rich period in your world's history, and not an altogether stable one.

In was during this period that the realm you know as Faerie came into being as a product of this liminal magic. When a line of possible humanity was rejected, it didn't just disappear. The spirits animating this line simply moved into the etheric and continued their development, becoming the giants and little people of legend. In some respects, Faerie is the fossil remnant of early humanity.

Of course, it is more than this, and because of its origins, its nature entwines both your people and ours. But though we are partly responsible for its emergence, and though there are those among us who participate in it and even have incarnated into Faerie forms—which in some cases are the cast off forms of early humanity—we are not Faerie beings.

Since some of the beings who live in Faerie are descendents or continuations of early competitors of yours, there can still be found a spirit of rivalry or even at times of jealousy and antipathy. Not all Faerie beings are automatically kindly disposed towards you.

Another difference is that the spirits and souls of many of those early experiments at humanity came out of Gaia; they are nature souls or earth souls, if I may call them this. They are more intimately aligned with the realm of the nature spirits than we are because they are part of it or it was their origin. It is not our origin, nor is it yours. As I said, this is why we think of them as children of Gaia.

The realm of Faerie is more wide-spread across your globe and more diverse in its manifestations than our realm. Many in this realm are true nature spirits, but others are hybrids, bearing in their lineage the energy and memory of being almost human. Many Faerie beings are simply ancient and alternate forms of humanity which died out or were pushed out of the physical realm but which continue their existence and development parallel to yours and to ours. They continue to stand in their own magic, even as you do in yours and we do in ours.

There is a task of reconciliation with the realms of Faerie, but it is of a different nature than the task between your people and mine. You never were part of their realm and thus did not split from it. While there are Faerie beings who can and do take incarnation as human individuals, as a species you draw your incarnational fire from a different source. The split you have with

Faerie is ecological and is part of the larger condition of separation that exists between you and the natural world around you.

In this time, many types of consciousnesses and lines of evolution and development seek to bring a new state of wholeness into being in keeping with changes in the subtle structure of the planet, but that is a topic for another time.

I feel this is enough for now.

Blessings!

STAR ENERGIES

Since Mariel discusses "star energies" a great deal, I asked her to give more definition to this idea. A couple of days passed in the class, and then she replied with the following long discussion.

Greetings! First, let me say that to us stars are not places; they are not points of light in the sky. They are beings which may hold within their fields of energy vast collectives of consciousness. This is true for our sun which is a star; it sounds its own note of consciousness, yet it also contains within its aura all the lives that you know of here on earth, both physical and non-physical, and many other types of lives of which you do not know. For none of the planets in the solar system are truly barren of life, though they may not support physical life as this world does. They are all home to beings of different constituencies and different evolutions than your own. All these lives in some manner add to and modulate the signature of energy and consciousness that is the contribution of our sun to the cosmos at this time.

Stars, including our sun, emit what in a human body would be trace minerals necessary to the metabolism of the whole, and in some cases, produce the energetic equivalent to enzymes and hormones vital to the function of cosmic systems of life. It truly is a case of "as above, so below", and the macrocosm is reflected in the microcosm. Thus, in a broad sense, stellar influences could be likened to metabolic chemicals that enable the living processes to proceed within many forms of life, from planets to atoms.

If the earth may be likened to an organ within the body of

the solar presence, then the sun is an organ within the body of a still larger system of consciousness and life. At the same time, certain other stellar sources are also organs within this same larger configuration. Their output affects the body of this greater life, but also affects our solar system and, both directly and indirectly, our planet.

So, in this context, there are stellar influences that act like hormones or enzymes making possible connections and processes that otherwise would not function properly if at all. In the simplest picture, they promote the coherency of the larger whole of which your earth and your sun and the other planets of this solar system are a part.

This is a cosmic picture. There is an individual side to this as well. There are many classes of lives that came to this world from the stars. Humanity and the Sidhe are among these. This means that there exists within us ancient connections to the various stellar sources from which we came. An analogy might be to say that within your bloodstream is salt that is a remnant of the ancient ocean from which your physical ancestors arose. You evolved from a salt-filled environment, and as a consequence, salt is necessary to your body and your life. In similar ways, certain stellar energies are necessary as well to your Souls and to ours.

However, because of the split between us, we remained in a more "stellar-rich" environment, while you entered into a physical world predominated by telluric, lunar and solar energies. You still need a touch of stellar energy but not as much as you require forces emanating from the sun, the moon, and the land beneath you.

We, on the other hand, have greater need of replenishment from stellar sources, which is one of the functions I perform as what you might think of as a stellar priestess. Just as the salt of the ancient earthly oceans is part of your blood, as well as the iron of the earth itself, so star energies are part of our blood. We need the connection to the stars as much as you need connection to sun, earth, and water. All of us have this connection, but some of us are trained to work with and mediate the life force of the stellar sources, drawing it directly into our world.

Remember, too, that our world is to some extent an unnatural one. It did not evolve as much as it was created by us, and the power to create and sustain it came from our stellar connections, our star-selves, if you wish. Thus, the substance of our world requires connection and infusion from those stars that are our sources. Those like myself work to be the bridges that nourish our land and each other with the stellar Light.

You do not need stellar energies in this same way, but you do need them. Historically, much of what you have needed has been provided by the sun and to a lesser degree by the moon, but the cosmic influence has been there as well. It is an "enzyme" vital to planetary life. Further, you require stellar energies for the growth and nourishment of your souls, for you, too, are part of the cosmic environment.

The stellar influence has been important in the development of your minds that raise you above the animal kingdom, and it is important in inspiring and empowering you to reach beyond the confines of the earth and the material realm into the wonder and spaciousness of larger possibilities. It opens you to a greater field of evolution and development. In effect, it allows you to be more than just a child of the earth. Your etheric bodies contain strands of stellar energy that give you a power of connection to more than just the energies of the earth.

In your history, these strands have exerted less influence than other strands of energy and connection taken from the planetary weave. Your task, you see, has been to become truly part of the earth. But now this is changing. The earth's own etheric structure is changing, weaving a new form for itself, one that contains more star-threads and thus a greater sensitivity to and connection with the cosmic environment beyond the sun. This is a vital change in the life history of Gaia; think of it as gaining an ability to hear star-songs that otherwise were too faint or too overwhelmed by the song of the sun and moon. What these star-songs contain is important for Gaia.

Your own etheric structures are embedded in that of Gaia, so this change affects you as well. Humanity is also weaving a new etheric body for itself, one in which the stellar threads have more prominence and new threads of stellar energies are added.

The main objective of this is not to enable you to hear star-songs more fully but to hear the star song within the earth more fully. In other words, while this change will make it easier for you to connect with stellar energies, the objective is not to draw you away from the earth but to enable you to blend more fully with it. It is to enable you to see and hear and be part of the "stars within the earth."

I realize these are just words or word pictures for you, but I trust if you ponder them, deeper understandings will come forth.

This growing prominence of stellar forces in the destiny of the world is one reason we need to come forward and find reconciliation with you. For we are proficient in knowing the stars, just as you are proficient in knowing the earth. What we hope is to blend with you in ways that will support the unfoldment of your own etheric changes, the birth of your own new etheric body. It's for this reason I have said we don't come to give you information about us but to form connections that will help you discover new aspects to yourself, to find once more in your being the star-soul that would bring new threads into your incarnational weaving.

This is enough for now. I shall add more later. My blessings to you and the blessings of the stars!

WAYS OF CONNECTING WITH STELLAR ENERGIES

After the preceding communication, I wondered if Mariel or her companions might have suggestions on how we might go about attuning to stellar energies and qualities. I got this reply.

Greetings! You ask how you might attune to the stellar forces that eternally flow to your world but now do so with increasing intensity. My first response must be to say that this is a subject that we, too, are exploring, so I cannot give you a definitive answer.

When I attune to the stars and draw their qualities into myself, allowing them to then flow into our world, I do so through my blood. As I have said, our blood is rich with stellar elements and qualities in a way analogous to how your blood is rich in the salt and minerals of the ancient oceans from which you come as a physical species. In a manner of speaking, there is a river of Light from the stars that is like a bloodstream flowing from the stellar beings into Gaia and hence into our world as well. It is a river of "star blood", if you will, and our blood resonates with it. Those like myself are trained to step into this flow and draw it into ourselves using this resonance with our own blood.

But your blood is different, even as your bodies are different from our own. Your physical substance has a more complex mixture of elements than does ours, which makes you more resonant physically with the forces of the sun, moon and earth than you are with the stars. Speaking generally, you must work harder than I do to find the stellar resonance within yourselves, but it is easier for you than it is for me to find the resonance with the earth. This is the result of our evolutionary histories, and it is why we can—and must—complement each other.

Though this oversimplifies the issue, I could say that we come to the stars through our blood and our substance but we come to nature and the world through our minds and our hearts. You, on the other hand—and again, I simplify—come to nature and the physical world through your blood and your substance but you come to the stars through your minds and hearts. In other words, it is an inner process for you, just as connecting with the natural world of the physical earth is in many ways an inner process for us.

The challenge is that humans come in such a wide variety. Some of you are closer to what we are and have your stellar heritage close to the surface of your being, whereas in others of you, it is deeply buried or present in a smaller percentage of elements compared to the richness of what you draw from the earth itself. Thus, what might work for one person as a form of stellar attunement would not work at all for another.

You are more of a synthesis than we are. This is your strength, and it is also a challenge, for in the midst of your synthesis of elements from the world, from the sun and moon, from the stars, and from the various kingdoms of life, you must discover the trace minerals, so to speak, that connect to the star streams. For some of you, this is easier done than for others, though all humans possess such traces. And you must do so without disrupting your capacity for synthesis. You must find a balance that honors all the elements of your nature without overemphasizing one to the detriment of the others.

So, underlying your request is the fact that there is exploration involved in discovering the answer that fits for you. I cannot give you a recipe. You must find the stars within yourself.

Having said this, however, I can make suggestions. I pass on to you these images of ways you may explore. Experiment with these practices and let us see what results. Remember, we are exploring as much as you.

Remember as well, the purpose is to draw the stellar forces into harmony and integration with your world, not to be drawn by them out to the stars. There is a potential for glamour here, for stellar forces contain much wonder and power; they are rich in magic. Remember that these are ordinary forces of the universe that are rising in your world the way a tide rises on a beach; it is a natural phenomenon, and we wish you to be natural with it.

Our blessings as always and with them, the blessings of the stars that shine upon us all.

At the conclusion of this message, Mariel passed on to me a series of images of exercises any of us could do to attune to stellar energies. These exercises do not exhaust the many possible ways in which a person might attune to the stars and their inner qualities; they are only a starting point.

The exercises are presented in Part III of the book.

THE NATURE OF MAGIC

At different times in her conversations with me, Mariel has mentioned a capacity which I have translated as "magic." Of course, the Sidhe are famous for being magical, and I have wanted for some time to ask her about this. What exactly does "magic" mean in this context? And are we not magical, too, in our own way?

The English occultist Dion Fortune defined magic as changes in consciousness brought about by the will, with the implication that these changes in consciousness would be reflected in some manner in events and actions in the physical world. Certainly, we have a collective image of the magician as one who wields secret powers and can bend the world to his or her will, creating miracles. Merlin, Gandalf, Dumbledore, Harry Potter—these are the major images of magicians (and of magic) in the popular imagination. But what was Mariel's understanding of this?

Greetings! You wish to explore the nature of magic in my world. For humans, magic is a form of control, a way of shaping the world around you in accordance with your wishes. This is true for us as well but to a much lesser extent. For us, magic is a skill of engagement and cooperation.

We shouldn't talk of magic as if it were one phenomenon. It is really many things bundled together into this single word. For instance, there is a magic of glamour and illusion which operates almost entirely in the realms of thought and desire. Humans are well-versed in this kind of magic as well, and its purpose is often manipulative, though whether for good or evil depends on the intent. In your world, this form of magic is performed through combinations of words, images, and actions that can trick the eye and beguile the mind and heart. In our world, it is as often performed directly through the mind in telepathic ways. If used with a human being, it can lead the individual to see and to feel what we suggest, weaving about them a skein of illusion.

In my world, this kind of magic is often used for performance and is considered a form of art. Normally, it is frowned upon as a tool of manipulation, but it can be used as such nonetheless. However, this magic cannot truly affect the world, nor is it a magic of engagement and cooperation. If you paint the color red upon a wall, it changes how the wall appears but it does not change what the wall is. It does not change its substance, nor does it bring you into deeper relationship with the wall itself. It is a surface thing, so we think of this kind of magic as surface magic.

Deep magic is something else. You think of magic as originating with the will and the mind, as in the definition you shared with me. But this kind of magic, while it can be effective in the right circumstances, is one of projection. It is like the light that casts your shadow onto the world. In the end, whatever you create, you remain yourself.

Deep magic changes us when we use it, and in a way, this is partly its purpose. It does not originate from our minds. It can be guided by our wills, but it originates first from our bodies and the life and spirit within them. It is a sharing—even a giving—of our life force to the world that together we may craft and shape something. And in this crafting, we are changed as well. The world enters us and lives in us. I suppose you could say that deep magic for us is a form of mating with the world, though there is nothing sexual about it. But it arises from our awareness—and our experience—of being embedded in and part of the world. Deep magic for us, then, is not acting upon the world as an isolated and separate identity but rather acting with the world in recognition of how our identities blend and contribute to each other.

The way deep magic changes us lies usually in strengthening our sense of oneness with the world. It takes us into a spaciousness that the world builds with us. It takes us into the presence of our larger Self.

Deep magic is a blending of ourselves, our life energies, our will, and the energies and life of the world. What results may be guided and shaped by our intelligence and desire, but it is something created in concert and harmony with the life within the world. It is a joint creation.

Understanding magic as a form of communion and engagement with the world, born of honoring and loving the world, means that we can live in magic. It is not just something we do, arising out of our will and desire. It is something we experience, something we are because of our relationship with the life of the world around us.

This is not an unknown state to you. You say, "I am in the flow", and everything seems to move gracefully around you. Synchronicities naturally happen without your needing to make them happen. You are in magic, living magic. You are being magic. This is what deep magic is all about.

If you approach magic as an art of control and manipulation, you will find certain forms of magic that allow this, as I have said, but they will be limited in scope and will ultimately limit you as well. They will not be the deep magic of which I speak.

If you approach magic as a living engagement of your body, your mind, your heart, your life energy with the world around you, you will find yourself slipping into the place of deep magic. If you give yourself to your world in a sharing of life and consciousness, you will find deep magic—the world's magic—rising up around you.

And you will be changed.

Blessings as always.

A TRIALOGUE ON THE SPECIES OF GAIA

As I've said, I've had contact and communication with the subtle worlds for most of my life. This is a different phenomenon for me that communicating with the Sidhe, though there are similarities since both deal with phenomena that are beyond the ordinary physical plane.

I regularly work in my writing and classes, and in my everyday research into the connections between our world and the subtle dimensions, with a group of beings whom I think of as my colleagues. Most of them were incarnate humans at one time or another. I don't normally name them since their actual names are embedded in their vibrational "feel"; that is, each of them has a signature energy that is distinctly individual. This is how I recognize them.

I had found the material that Mariel had brought up about the origins of Faerie and the different sub-species of human beings, some of which were continuing to evolve upon a non-physical wavelength of existence, to be interesting and provocative. As a consequence, one morning I began discussing it with one of my subtle colleagues, whom I'll call "Phillip" for convenience. During this conversation, Mariel appeared and joined in, making it not a dialogue but a "trialogue." I have attempted to reproduce it below.

David: Here is the issue. I have experienced nature spirits of various kinds. I have experiences with subtle beings like you, Phillip. I have on rare occasions encountered what I think of as Faerie beings, such as the elven individual I encountered once on the lawn at a conference center in Seattle. And now for the past few years, I've had contact with the Sidhe, largely through you, Mariel. While there are some similarities to these encounters, the "vibe" has been very different between them as well.

I understand that the Sidhe are neither subtle beings as you are, Phillip, nor nature spirits, and I don't think they are entirely Faerie beings either. It seems to me there is a whole other ecosystem here, maybe many more than one. Any comments?

Phillip: This is correct. Gaia is home to many streams of evolution and life. Humanity and Sidhe are only two points along a continuum. Nor are the edges between the different streams always hard boundaries. Overlap is possible such that at times it may be difficult for you to determine to which stream a particular individual belongs.

You make a distinction between incarnate and subtle beings, though you understand that I, a subtle being, feel myself to be incarnated in my particular domain. Still, it's a useful distinction. We would define the difference in this way. A subtle being is a direct expression of its identity; that is, its body is usually a manifestation of its core identity. What you see is who the being is.

An incarnate being, on the other hand, is a mediated identity. Its body of expression is formed by other entities who mediate and participate in the expression of the incarnating or organizing identity. Thus, you have a physical body made up of cells that are lives in their own right separate from your own. You have subtle bodies that are made up to a greater or lesser degree of energies that do not originate with your soul but are drawn from the world.

I think of myself as incarnated, but my body, which is solid to me but seems made of insubstantial energy to you, is still a direct expression of my consciousness, spirit and life. So by my own distinction, I am a subtle being as I am unmediated in my manifestation.

David: Yes, this is how I understand it. This is a basic concept in Incarnational Spirituality, though I have never used the term "a mediated identity" to describe incarnation. I like this! It's very helpful. Thank you!

Phillip: You're welcome! What is important to understand is that a being can be incarnated in the sense of having a mediated identity and still not be physical in your terms. Or perhaps I should say it need not be solid to be incarnated. Because of this, there is a wide continuum of different types of beings—what you might call species—that are incarnated or mediated forms of life. Because most of them inhabit bodies made up of subtler substances than yours, you may think of them as subtle or spirit beings, but they are not, at least not as we are defining things here.

David: And as I understand it, the purpose of this "mediation," of wearing substances made up of lives and identities other than our own, is to further the development of these lives?

Phillip: Yes, as well as your own. This is a beneficial side effect for the beings involved in doing the mediation. Learning how to hold a diversity of intelligences within yourself, is itself important, but in addition, when you are in touch with your identity, you release a Light that blesses all who share and co-create your bodies with you.

At this point, Mariel made an appearance to join in the conversation.

Mariel: We are among those who are incarnated but are not densely physical as you are, David. We are also kin to you because we are both star-born in our natures. This is not true for all those who share what you are calling the continuum of incarnation. Many are more properly called the Children of Gaia. They originate from Gaia's own creative desires and expression and are the products of her evolution. We also are familiar with and work with the realm of Faerie, sometimes quite closely. For us, they truly are Gaia's children. They are Gaia exploring herself through various forms and patterns of life.

Phillip: Yes, Life can originate from many sources and develop in different directions. It does not always fit into neat categories. Rather than trying to explain it or make it conform to a taxonomic system, you should consider each life in its own terms within its own ecology of connections.

Mariel: I have already described that there were different experiments in the development of humanity, most of which did not succeed. But some of them continue to evolve within subtler dimensions of incarnation.

David: My impression from what both of you are saying is that the realm of Faerie is a realm of incarnation made up of these Gaian evolutions, including other, older forms of humanity.

Phillip: This is partly correct. Faerie is a human term, and it covers a wide variety of manifestations. Often when someone doesn't know where to put a particular phenomenon, it's relegated to the realm of Faerie. Faerie beings are on the whole an evolutionary stream unto themselves, one rooted in Gaia's life and emerging from her womb, so to speak. But there are also nature spirits who work with this stream who take on many aspects of Faerie. It is not easy for most humans to distinguish between them.

Mariel: You will remember that I said that all incarnate beings are accompanied by symbiotic and collaborative subtle beings designed to help foster their development. Sometimes what you encounter as faeries are the subtle beings accompanying us or accompanying you—and sometimes they are beings paired with another stream of evolution. As your colleague says, it is not easy to tease them apart.

Phillip: Just as there are species of physical animals and plants only found in certain geographical locations, so there are non-material beings, both incarnate and subtle, who have evolved out of and are generally tied to certain geographical locations and features of your world. Think of the angel of a particular landscape or the nature spirits dedicated to a particular place. Though it is not always so, there may be an incarnate equivalent to these beings. You think of incarnation as a descent from a higher level, but it can work the other way, that the spirits of a river, a lake, a mountain, a particular landscape can take on an incarnate form, not in the dense matter that you wear but in etheric or astral forms.

David: Such incarnations would then be limited to this area?

Phillip: Essentially, yes. You might think of them as a local species, not a planetary one. For this reason, you should always factor place into how you recognize and think about these beings. If they are planetary in nature and beyond place, this will become apparent. But place is where you start in your understanding.

Mariel: But what you need to realize is that all these manifestations are magical, even as you are, though you do not see yourselves as magical. Think of magic as the capacity to widen the spectrum of possibility, allowing more manifestations and outcomes to be capable of emergence than might happen otherwise..

You make much of faerie magic. This is often the magic of a place acting through those deeply attuned to it, those who are embodying the life of this place. Such beings, incarnate in an etheric realm, may seem very magical to you because even though "mediated" as your colleague says, they are part of the circulation of life within the land they occupy. They can seem like gods or goddesses at times because of the power that emerges from their connectedness.

Phillip: Yes, this is true. And as Mariel says, you are also magical in this way. The challenge of humanity is that you are mediated on many levels; your connection to the earth and to the stars becomes lost in the "noise" of many voices speaking within you and as you. You lose your own voice. So you must regain a sense of your identity but also of your connections. You must find how you are connected through your identity rather than through the mediations that represent you but are not you.

David: In other words, my body has a connection to the land around me, but that is the body's connection; it's a mediated connection, so to speak. What I must do is enrich and add to this connection through an act of deliberate, mindful, willing attunement and love.

Phillip: Yes. Your body's connections are powerful but also very ancient. They are like old channels through which you wish to pump fresh, new water.

Mariel: This is part of how we can help you. We are not as "mediated" as you. Our identities shine through our outer coverings more fully. This is not because we are more advanced. It is because we have not entered into matter and covered ourselves in its substances as fully as you. So we can add our energy to yours and we can remind you of who you are so that you can stand in a more cosmically-aligned identity and from there connect to your world through all the layers of your "mediation". By remembering how you are of the stars, you can understand how to be more fully of the earth.

Phillip: I would leave you on this note. I have nothing more to add to what my colleague has just said. Except perhaps this, which is only an affirmation of what you have already experienced and already know. Gaia herself is a mediated identity, and you are part of this mediation. Just as you wish your own body to be whole, Gaia wishes this for her life as well, and you, along with all the other species that form the bodies of this world, are instruments of this wholeness.

The world in its entirety, incorporating physical and non-physical dimensions, is complex and filled with endless forms of life. None of your maps wholly capture this, and perhaps no map will. So you can encounter many strange and wondrous types of inner life. Whether you call them Faerie or not, or whatever you call them, remember that they are mediating the world with you, and in the end they are no stranger, no more miraculous, no more magical than you are yourself.

NOTE: My wife, Julia, hearing about this experience, asked me what it was like. After all, Mariel and Phillip exist on two different wavelengths, yet obviously they were aware of each other, and I'm on a different wavelength from either of them. For me, the experience was like having one of them standing on one side of me and the other on the other side, but both were held in a mental and etheric "bubble" or space that was part of my own subtle energy field. While I suppose it's entirely possible that Phillip and Mariel could be independently aware of each other, in this case, I was the link between them.

Over the years, I've created a specialized field of subtle energies that I call my "alliance space" or "contact space." It's like a special room where non-physical beings and I can meet and connect. Part of my challenge initially in relating to Mariel was that she did not use this "inner room" to contact and communicate with me—and for the most part, still does not do so. But in this instance, she entered into the "room" with Phillip and me so that the three-way conversation could take place, with all parties aware of each other.

THE FAERIE REALMS AND BEYOND

The question of the nature of the Faerie realms and their relationship to the Sidhe was one that had "legs" in the class as an ongoing topic of discussion. There were participants who had years of shamanic training and practice and who often encountered strange and wondrous beings of one kind or another, beings that clearly weren't Sidhe but weren't subtle beings, either. Were they part of Faerie or something else. The trialogue with Phillip and Mariel only seemed to whet participants' appetites to ask more questions. Mariel tried to oblige.

Greetings! You present me with questions, and I am glad to answer what I can within the protocols that guide our contact and collaboration.

What you must understand is that life is wild, and this is true on our side of the veil as much as on yours. If there is a niche

112

which life can fill, if there is a pattern that life can explore, if there is a potential that life can unfold, it will attempt to do so.

There are certain broad categories in which you attempt to define and classify subtle life. You speak of angels, Devas, elementals, nature spirits, fairies, elves, and of course, of us, the Sidhe, as well as many other beings that have arisen within your cultural folklore and histories. While such categories can be useful, not everything fits neatly within them, or even fits at all. Further, as planetary conditions evolve and change, new "species" of beings are always appearing, some, in fact, brought into existence by you as you create new energy environments and patterns around yourself through your thoughts, your imaginations, and your creative and technological actions. [I would call these anthropogenic beings, subtle entities created by the inner and outer actions of humanity—David].

With this in mind, what you term Faerie is a broad category indeed that encompasses many types of subtle life and consciousness. And we recognize that at times you include us in this category as well.

It seems to us, though you would know better than we do, that, while nature spirits deal with the inner processes of life and form, the "nuts and bolts" as you might say, what you mean by Faerie are beings that possess and express what to you are magical qualities and abilities. It is the magical dimension of Faerie more than its nature connections that seems to attract and beguile you as incarnate human beings, which is understandable given that you have a racial memory of and longing for your own innate magical capacities. This gives Faerie a glamour in your thinking that the routine work of the Devas and nature forces may not possess. I am speaking generally, of course, but this is how it looks to us.

How we define the beings and forces of Faerie, then, may not be the same as how you define them since we are looking at this from different perspectives. It is not the magical side that stands out for us in the way it does for you since we are well aware of the magic we possess, which is why you consider us magical beings as well.

Broadly speaking, the Faerie realm to us is equivalent to what you speak of as the indigenous or native peoples of the planet. They are beings who live close to and entwined with the living forces of the planet. They are not necessarily nature spirits, though they may work closely with them—indeed, many of them are not "spirits" at all but are beings engaged, even as we are, in modes of incarnation that lie at the edge of the physical world but not wholly in it. Some of them are even more physically incarnate than we are, though not as much as you.

There are two lines of Faerie, those that are directly and completely Children of Gaia, manifestations and incarnations of the planet's own evolutionary forces, and those that spring out of the experiments in developing the human species. Of these latter, there are two further divisions, for humanity arises from two distinct impulses. There is that branch of humanity, of which you and I are representative, whose consciousness was stimulated by stellar forces and whose souls have their origins amidst the stars. Then there is a parallel branch whose consciousness was quickened and heightened by angels and Devas working as part of Gaia. So you could say there was a stellar humanity and a planetary humanity. The boundaries between the two were not—and are not—hard and fast, for there was cross-fertilization between the two. Further, before the world became as fully material as it is now, there were different experiments of form within each line, sometimes inspired by developments in the other line.

As time progressed, many of these forms of humanity discontinued their wholly physical existence but continued to develop, though not as quickly, within the subtle realms. These "planetary humans" are loved by Gaia and are close to her; they are often the "little people" or the "forerunners" that are spoken of in your legends and folklore.

The issue is complicated by the fact that many of the Children of Gaia, the Faerie folk that are their own line of development and not part of humanity in any respect, are natural mimics. Their own natural shape is often highly malleable, and they are masters of illusion. They mimic humanity and they also mimic our people, the Sidhe. This can blur the lines between Faerie, Sidhe and humanity. There are also Faerie beings—and subtle beings as well—that inhabit thought forms created by humanity. So, if you encounter a tall elven being with pointed ears and a bow, are you encountering a Faerie, a Sidhe, or a humanly engendered thought-form animated by human collective energies or perhaps by a subtle being or even one of the Faerie races?

In addition, certain of the great planetary elemental beings—lords of stone and water, fire and air—can take human form and interact with you, especially if the human being is attuning to and working with the elemental forces which they inhabit and control.

Even we Sidhe, though we have deep ancestral connections with you and share with you stellar origins, take different forms. Some of us live closer to you and to nature, others further away. The Sidhe are no more homogeneous than you are as a species, so you cannot categorize us as one thing or another.

So my advice is you should not jump to conclusions but allow a contact to unfold its deeper nature for you. Be cautious with labels and with premature naming. Remember as well that it's not who or what a being is that is the most important but the nature of the relationship that you form with it and the consequences that flow from this connection.

This is enough for now. I shall speak with you again later. Blessings as always and joy!

STARLIGHT – EARTHFIRE

As the class reached its midway point, I began to "hear" on the inner a particular refrain. It seemed at times to come from Mariel and at times just generally from the Sidhe. It repeated itself several times. It said, "We bring Starlight, you bring Fire."

I mentioned this to Jeremy, and he produced the following two paintings. If you look closely above the opening in each Stone, there is a kneeling figure tending the stars and the fire.

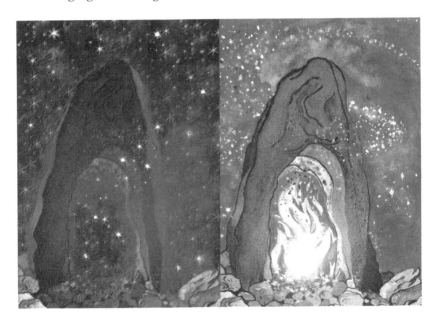

"WE BRING STARLIGHT — YOU BRING FIRE"

After I posted these pictures online on the class site for others to enjoy, I had a short message from Mariel:

> The fire you bring to the world is that of love. For you to find your loving place, the center within from which you love not just as an emotion but as a force of wholeness and nourishment, can be a more difficult process for you than for us, as more stands in your way. A diamond found lying on the ground is beautiful and a joy to find, but a diamond dug out from deep within the earth

has the same beauty but reflects as well the power and effort that went into the digging. Our world is strewn with diamonds; the Light of the Lover is plain to us. But in your world you must dig, which makes the presence of love in you so much more potent. We are attracted to your power of love and are warmed by it. Think of us when you go to your loving place and invite us to share it with you.

With this message, I began to sense something that Mariel was trying to communicate that went deeper than the subject matter we'd been discussing, something suggested by the pictures above and by the phrase, "We bring starlight, you bring fire." There was something very important here that she wanted to convey. Slowly it began to surface through the last half of the class.

A GLIMPSE OF MARIEL'S LIFE AND WORK

The class was half over, and I was feeling every time I contacted Mariel a small degree of frustration and even urgency. When we would attune to each other, I would catch glimpses in the back of her mind that she was not making the contact with the class as a whole that she wished, and as a consequence, some of her energy was not getting through. I wasn't sure what to do about this, and it troubled me.

Then one morning (Mariel usually contacted me early in the morning when my mind was fresh), I sensed a distinct change. Something had shifted for her, and it was reflected in her conversation with me. Up till then, she had been adamant about not sharing much about herself or about the Sidhe in general; she didn't want to become the focus. But she must have decided that this was a mistake, for in the message that morning, she became more self-revealing than I had known her to be in all the years we had been conversing.

Greetings!
Let me tell you something of myself and of my life.
In my world, I live in two places. I have a home in a small community. We live in what you would call a rural area, close to a forest. We are not in the forest, though we often spend time there. Our community is in an open area, a meadow, and a river runs nearby. There are numerous hills in the area where I live, some bare, some with clusters of trees at their summit. All are within easy walking distance from our homes. In the distance is a range of mountains, and one of our cities lies near the base of one of these mountains.

I go there to the city occasionally both for work and for pleasure, and when there, I have friends with whom I stay. I am part of an association that holds lodgings in the city for those who may need it when they visit or if they stay to do a piece of work, but I seldom use them unless I have a need for solitude.

My second residence, if you would call it such, is a small structure—I think you might think of it as a temple— where I perform many of my duties as a priestess. It is on a hill surrounded by trees, not far from our community. It is a round structure and would remind you of one of your astronomical observatories, save that the roof of the dome is open to the sky and stars. In the center is a well, and above it is a platform where I may sit and attune to the forces which I mediate. There is a room where I may sleep and prepare meals during the times I am in residence, and there is a room where I may hold consultation with those who visit me. There is also a room with an altar, around which are arranged small alcoves for meditation.

I am not the only one who uses this temple; there is a group of us in our community who take turns being in residence. If there are ceremonies that involve our community, there is space near and around this temple for many to gather. In one of our ceremonies, one of us invokes the star energies to which this temple is dedicated and draws them into the water of the well, from whence it flows out into the land. We also drink and share the water from the well at such times, drawing the star forces into our bodies as well.

Most of my community, though not all, are part of the association I mentioned. We are all priests and priestesses, but in our land, this does not have the same religious connotations it has for you. It means we mainly work as counselors and healers, and in the process act as mediators of spiritual forces. And unlike your priests, we are trained to move through more than one dimension in the quest of knowledge and understanding. My community is particularly strong in this regard. We see ourselves as a community of researchers and explorers, which is why we have undertaken this work with you. Of course, we are not isolated in this work but are in touch with many who share our interests and seek greater collaboration with humanity.

Since this work with you began, both in my home in the community and in the temple, I have created a special altar space that is dedicated to my connection with you. This altar reflects the true altar which is in my heart. Here I "make space" for you in my life. Here I sit in silence and connect with your human energies, and what I learn or experience, I bring back and instill into this altar. This altar is only partly solid; it is a blend of energy and substance. When I bring back experience and memory to it, it changes its colors to reflect what has been added. Each time I touch your energies, I bring something back to add.

This altar is an outward reflection of my connection with you. It creates a "sphere of humanity" around itself to which I may attune. In so doing, I strengthen my ability to enter and engage with your world. It is an outward manifestation of my portal to you.

When I use this altar, I do so by first attuning to what I am both as Sidhe and as star priestess. It is important that I carry into the presence of this altar the depths of my own being. I bring myself—my attuned self—to you. I go to the place of love that is the heart of my life and being as priestess, for all the connections I make—with stars, with the land, with others—is through love and an acknowledgement of the common love that we share. Though you may not fully understand the distinction, I do not come to you as a priestess, for that role would be an obstacle between us, but I must stand in my sacredness and priestliness in order to come to you. It is love that bridges the dimensions.

The card deck we inspired you to create can be your equivalent in your world to my altar, though again the real "altar" is in your heart. The cards were, as I have said, designed to create a portal. Whether you use it or not, I would still encourage you, if you wish communion and contact with us, to make space for us in your life. Stand in your own loving sacredness, your own priestliness, and attune to us. Take time to make space for us in your heart.

When I come to you, the agenda is to connect, nothing more. Anything else will unfold out of the connection. I suggest the same at your end. Do not summon us with a mind filled with needs or tasks for which you seek our help. Just be in the fire of your love and invite us to join you and warm ourselves. Let our starlight meet your heartfire. Stand in your sacredness so our sacredness may connect. If there are tasks to do or needs to be met or help we may give, it will unfold out of the connection.

Go to your inner temple and invite us in, just as I go to my temple and invite you in. Make space for us, and everything else will follow.

MARIEL'S TEMPLE

When transcribing the previous message, there came a point at which I was uncertain what I was being shown. Was Mariel's temple on top of a hill in the midst of a grove of trees or was it in a clearing in the forest? I kept seeing both and at times they would superimpose, which was confusing. Eventually, like Schrodinger's famous cat in quantum physics, I chose one image over the other based only on the logic that it was a star temple and thus wouldn't it be on a hill, closer to the stars? Still, I wasn't satisfied. I also came away feeling there was more she had wanted to say—or something I had missed—or both—but by the end, I couldn't hang on to the contact as my energy had dwindled. But a few hours later, she came back, laughing, and had this to say:

You got the descriptions half right. You need to trust your first impressions, though I understand why it was confusing. You live in a world in which things are one way or another, but this is not our world. Forms are rarely so permanent or fixed. You got most of my temple right, but you are trained to think in terms of "buildings" which for you usually are permanent structures.

Not so for us. Our buildings are alive, brought into being partly, as I said once long ago, by our singing and dancing. They are not alive as a creature would be, but they are expressions of sentient energy and thus are responsive to our living presence and our thoughts. In a way not possible for you, our buildings are only partly solid. They are energy patterns into which we weave starlight and moonlight, sunlight and earthlight, and of course, our own Sidhe-light; when we need an aspect of this structure to be solid, it is. There are principles of connection that govern this process of building and manifestation, and these principles are as solid to us as your laws of physics and material structure are to you. Buildings once brought into being cannot be manipulated merely by whim, unless they have been constructed with whimsy in mind. The form becomes anchored in the world, and we must respect this as much as you respect the hardness of a brick or the solidity of a plank of lumber.

Having said this, my temple is mobile. It is constructed in such a way that it can be easily shifted into an immaterial, dream-like state and then re-materialized where needed. So, at times it is indeed on the top of one of our hills and at times it is in the depths of the forest. It depends entirely on the nature of the energies and contacts with which I or my colleagues are working. Within certain limits, it can be larger or smaller in one place or another, again depending on the need, but it is not subject to whimsy nor can it take just any shape or any size.

So you see, you were correct in what you saw, but you felt it needed to be a choice, as it would be on your earth, whereas to me, both states—and others besides—are encompassed in the structure and composition of the temple. As I said at another time, our atoms hold multiple states of possibility at once. The temple is as much a creation of spirit, energy and possibility as it is of form.

Yes, there was more I wished to say. I am feeling delightfully verbal today, and the alignments between your world and mine are particularly close and free-flowing today. But for now I shall add only this:

I understand your wish to bring the class to a conclusive climax and the need to tie all things up in a nicely formed bow, but remember, this class is just a first step and in some ways a baby step. Just in holding it and creating this channel between your world and ours, much has been accomplished. We were not sure how it would unfold and manifest. As it is, it has turned out better than we had hoped. The field we wished to create encompassing all of you who are participating has indeed come into being, and yes, you are all woven into my altar. I realize that you each experience this differently, and some do so more acutely than others. This is the way of things. But rest assured you are all connected, and each connection is like a seed from which more can unfold if it has the space and nurturing to do so.

We would like you not to think of us as a "phenomenon". We are people like yourselves. Yes, there are differences, and some of the differences are significant—and I mean more than that you are more physical than we—but we are not wonder-workers or strange beings from another place. We are people sharing this world with you. This is why I suggested that when you think of us and reach out to us—when you make space for us—you do so with an open heart and mind not filled with projections or needs, desires or glamour.

Let us meet in the place where we can just sit together and be warmed in each other's fires, ours from the heart of stars, yours from the heart of earth. If you surround us with thought-forms, it is more difficult for us to meet you cleanly and clearly. If we have room to be ourselves in your life and are not constrained to fulfill a particular image or purpose, then we have the freedom—you would say the "elbow-room"—to bring what we are into your life in appropriate and perhaps for both of us, surprising ways. Likewise, I and my companions seek to hold you in such an open way, free from the images and thoughts that so often surround humanity.

Let us meet through love, and all else will unfold from this.

MOTHERING AND FAMILIES

Mother's Day occurred while the class was running, and this led to questions about parenting, children, and families among the Sidhe. One participant asked me, "Is Mariel a mother? Should we be celebrating her today, too?" At this point, Mariel was checking in with me every day. When she heard of these questions, she was delighted and proceeded to give me an answer.

Greetings! I join with you in celebrating the day you have set aside to honor the art of motherhood and those who practice this art. I am aware of your questions about motherhood and children amongst my people.

We also celebrate the spirit of motherhood that is part of the life of this world. We recognize the Mother as one of the faces of the divine and honor this face wherever and however it appears, for it transcends biology and is not bound to a single gender. Amongst my people, the capacity to bear and nourish children is one thing, but the capacity to embody the spirit of the Mother is something else.

You ask if I am a mother. I am what you might call a "participant mother." I have not born children through my own body. This may yet occur, but up to now, my work has precluded this. For us, the process of assisting a soul into form has biological and non-biological aspects. We have sexual union just as you do, though the call to mating is not as insistent nor all consuming as it is for you. But the womb into which a soul enters as it becomes part of our physical world is more than what the woman provides. It is an energy field that is held by several individuals united in a bond of love and communion together. Thus a child will have two biological parents but may also have several participant or energetic parents. I have been one of these and have participated in creating and holding such an energy womb. I have a son and a daughter who are children of my soul if not of my body. It is in this way that I know motherhood.

In my part of our world, there are few "nuclear" families such as you know them. Our families are more like clans, and thus a single child may have several who act as mothers and fathers. The relationship between a child and a non-biological parent is as close, and may in some instances be closer, than the relationship with a biological parent. This is because biology is not as powerful a determining factor in our lives as it is in yours. In our lives and relationships, we are more aware than you of the energetic or subtle components of our existence. Thus, two may mate physically but a larger mating takes place energetically among several who are called to this bonding. For us, this larger communion has more meaning and normally will take precedence over the physical sexual union.

This is not to diminish the power of the physical bond or the love that is expressed through it. It is to say that our lives and relationships are lived out simultaneously on several levels of consciousness and energy.

Whether a child is raised solely or mainly by his or her biological parents or is part of a communal clan with participant mothers and fathers depends on the child's needs and on other factors that may be present. There are souls that require a more focused field of attention. This may be particularly true if the soul itself is new to our race and does not have any history of being a Sidhe or any pattern of prior connections. For example, just as there are Sidhe that may take birth as a human being amongst your people, the reverse can also occur.

There are other reasons as well why a focused family unit may be the best environment for a particular child. The soul's needs are read prior to birth, and provisions are made accordingly. But most of our children are raised in a communal fashion, exposed to many nurturing and formative influences.

You are correct in understanding that we do not have many children. We are long-lived, so the need to replace members of the population who have gone on to other realms is not as urgent as it is with you. So the birth of a child is an event to be celebrated.

Childhood is different with us than it is with you, as well. There is no fixed number of years in which childhood takes place. Our bodies do not develop in the same way as yours since our bodies are more malleable and more reflective to our thought. Childhood for us is more a matter of the energy of the mind and heart than it is of the body, and an older soul will develop into adulthood physically faster than a younger one. It is possible that a soul will need an extended childhood—which may be one reason for it to be held, at least for a time, within an environment made up primarily of its biological parents. Such a child will develop slowly and will remain childlike in form for a longer period than one whose development of presence and identity is faster.

Thus a child may reach full maturity as an adult, both in mind and in body, much faster for us than for you where a child's physical pattern must follow strict biological rules and processes. On the other hand, if needed, a particular individual may remain a child in body for much longer than would happen in your world.

Is there romance amongst us? There is love, certainly, but we do not have the same kind of emotional bodies as you do. Romance for us is rarely an attraction or impulse of the body. We do not experience emotion in the same way as you, though we may experience the same qualities of emotion. We are more quicksilver in our feelings—they come and go more rapidly than they do for you, unless we will it otherwise. We can choose to become as emotionally involved as you, but it is rare.

On the whole, I believe you would find us less emotional than you. Some of us you would probably describe as "impersonal" or even "cold", though we may not be any less loving. It is the difference in the substance of our emotional bodies and how waves of emotional energy are propagated and held within them. It is the difference, say, between a wave moving through a body of water and one moving through a body of molasses. Emotions affect you more powerfully than they do us, though we can have quick bursts of feeling that are more intense than what you experience; your emotions last longer for you than ours do for us.

We relate more through our minds and spirits. We are not more spiritual than you in this regard, but we express through different frequencies of energy. You can find our presence disturbing because of this.

We form deep attachments to each other, and where children are concerned, we love and treasure them deeply and willingly form the bonds necessary for their whole development. But our attachments are not as based in emotion. Though it is a caricature, it is not too off the mark to say that the fictional character of the Vulcan Spock is unconsciously modeled after us. But we are not purely beings of mind or logic. We are emotional. We just carry the energies of emotion differently than you do.

Mothering is an important principle to us, so we are glad to join with you in honoring it and celebrating it. The practice of motherhood is different for us than for you—we do not define motherhood as much by biology and reproduction as you do—but its essence remains the same: to nurture and love the child and to do all that is necessary to enable it to fulfill its soul promise.

MARIEL'S ASSOCIATION

After the last message, I asked Mariel a follow-up question, as there were some elements to what she had said that I felt I had not properly registered at the time. In particular, I wondered if the two male Sidhe who often companioned her were related to her as I had sensed that one of them might be the soul-son she had mentioned. I was also curious about her soul-daughter. In a curious way, it seemed that I knew her, too, though I could not have said why I had that feeling. Mariel graciously responded and in the process had more to say about the "association" of which she is a part. As she related this information, I received a surprise.

Yes, as you have intuited, I am the participant-mother of one of the companions who accompany me. Our closeness makes him ideal in helping me make the energy transitions necessary to connect with you in this way.

I am interested that you ask about my soul-daughter. You have sensed her presence within my own energy field, have you not? We do the same work, and at times, she is the one who makes the link with you, though it is my thoughts and voice that you hear. This is part of her training but it is also true that at times, she is more suited in her youth to make the transitions into your realm that I am. Or else I am needed elsewhere and cannot give your realm the fullness of my attention. At such moments, she is my proxy.

This explained something to me. Although for me there is a sense of timelessness about the Sidhe that I have encountered—they are, after all, very long-lived, if not immortal—when Mariel had first come to me to work on the card deck, I felt her to be like an elder. The sense of wisdom around her seemed ancient to me, though admittedly I had little to go on to make any kind of comparison. She felt experienced and competent. As she herself alluded to in an earlier message, there was a moment when I wondered if she might be the Queen of the Sidhe since I felt this sense of dignity, nobility and wisdom around her. At the same time, her energy was youthful and vibrant. Judging her age, therefore, was difficult for me and not really that important.

However, as time went by, there were times when she felt younger to me, more like someone just starting out than someone with a rich accumulation of experience and wisdom. For a long time, I just put this down to the inconsistency of my own attunement and to my inexperience in working with the Sidhe. It wasn't a consistent thing, anyway, but it did make me feel that Mariel was showing me two distinct sides of her personality.

When she mentioned about her soul-children, though, I had a flash of intuition in which I saw a younger figure superimposed over Mariel. This seemed like another individuality altogether but one that was intimately close to Mariel. This is why I thought it might be her soul-daughter.

I did not know that you were aware of her as she holds herself in the background and is silent to allow my thoughts to come clearly through the medium of her consciousness. But you are correct that I work closely with my soul-daughter, and we share many of the same tasks and objectives.

This is not by accident. There is a reason why these two souls, for whom I am a participant mother, have been born amongst us and are part of our lives. I have said I am part of an association. It has existed for several hundreds of your years, and it was formed to create a foundation for the work we are doing now. It is an association dedicated to restoring wholeness upon the earth through reconciliation and partnership with human beings. In some ways, we are like a research program since we are also exploring just how this reconciliation and cooperation may come about, but we are also under the aegis of powerful spiritual forces who are agents of Gaia and who seek to further the wholeness of her life—and of all life—in this time of change. This is why there is some truth to considering us priests and priestesses.

There have been souls seeking birth amongst us to take part in this work. There are those in our association who have volunteered to be their parents and others of us who are happy and willing to join with them as participants in the larger womb of spirit through which these souls join us. So you see, our work has been developing for many years, even centuries, of your time, time enough for children to be born and to develop to take their roles in our endeavor, bringing with them the particular gifts of their souls.

Our association also has links to the human subtle worlds, and there are human souls who work with us, though not by taking birth as Sidhe—this would be too difficult for them. Their need to adapt and learn new ways of being would render them helpless and useless for the work we are doing. But as souls working from the inner planes of the world, they can add their wisdom and experience to ours and provide helpful advice and energy. You might think of them as consultants, and we value their presence and cooperation. What you do not realize is that some of those who are part of the inner group with whom you work are also participants in our association. I see that this surprises you. It is one of the links between us.

Beyond our association, though, we seek to bring into being a new order of co-workers, Sidhe and human and other beings as well, who will wear the mantle of service to the Earth, to Gaia, and to the cause of wholeness within all the kingdoms of life, seen and unseen. This is nothing more than the larger kinship of Gaian life, and it is this that we seek to join with you in serving.

MARIEL'S MOUNTAIN

This message is a "left-over." Communicating with Mariel was like plunging into a flowing river of words, concepts, impressions, images, and meaning. There would be a central current which was the main thrust of the message; that which Mariel most wished to convey. But at the same time, I would be aware of "currents" or tributaries off to the side carrying information that was part of the whole — part of the river — but in the background or moving off in interesting but non-essential directions that diverged from the main flow.

Sometimes, I could capture the whole river in my consciousness, but if it was a particularly long or complex communication, some of these side-impressions would be lost. Afterward, I might try to recapture them but often with no luck. They were simply gone. But sometimes, if I left it alone like not trying too hard to remember a dream, the information would show up unexpectedly, usually when I was thinking about something else or doing something entirely unrelated. I thought of these as left-over bits of the communication that had taken awhile to finally register.

I shared a communication that came during the class which I called "A glimpse of Mariel's life and work." The following is a left-over bit of this communication. I knew at the time there was more to the message than I'd been able to hold in my consciousness, but I couldn't retrieve it. This bit suddenly showed up three weeks after the class ended. When it did, it was as if I were back in touch with Mariel again — though in fact she wasn't around — and re-experiencing that earlier message, but this time with the missing bit front and center. It had to do with what she had described as her city and the mountain behind it.

I place it here in the book since it seems a logical continuation of the thread we've been following.

The city that is my second home is near a range of mountains and one mountain in particular. This mountain overlooks the land where I live and work and is a significant force in our lives. In many ways, it is a principle ally upon whose energy I particularly draw as it is a major conduit through which the energies of stars and earth meet.

I have said that I spend some time in the city. I do so for recreation, for in the culture it provides, it offers much for upliftment and renewal. Though they are very different from yours, we have our equivalents to your theater and music and art, though for us they are usually more participatory than for you. We seldom simply sit and watch.

The city, though, has another function in my life. It is itself a major conduit for energies drawn from the mountain, and it serves for me as what you might call a "base camp" for times when I make pilgrimage into the mountain for regeneration and amplification of my capacity to be a conduit myself for the stellar forces. These are important times for me of communion with the spirit of the mountain, whom I regard as one of my primary teachers and mentors.

Let me explain what a mountain is for us. Though it can certainly appear as a physical mountain such as you have in your world, it is for us not a geographical feature as much as a presence and an energy field. Your mountains are created through geological pressures and upheavals in the movement of your continental plates. Ours are created by the choice and actions of one of the great attendants of Gaia, a being you might call an angel or a Deva. Such a being may come on its own initiative, establishing itself in our world and entering into cooperation with us. It becomes one of the Great Ones helping to maintain and nurture our world, a gift from Gaia. Or it may come at the request of a number of us gathered together to invite its presence and to enter into a relationship with it with the objective of gaining its help.

Thus, a mountain for us is not an up thrusting of the earth from below as a result of geological pressures but a descent of a planetary spirit from its domain into our own. A mountain is thus a manifestation of purpose and intent, either its own or in collaboration with us. They thus provide points of contact for us with powerful spiritual beings and forces.

Some are more accessible than others. There are those few mountain spirits that prefer to be left alone as they are doing their work in deep solitude, and we respect this. Most, though, are happy to engage with us and work with us.

Our mountain is one of those created by invocation and invitation. I have spoken of our association. It grows out of a much older lineage of which I am a part, a lineage of those who work with star energies in one way or another. Millennia ago, many of us came together to create a part of our world dedicated to this work. We sought Gaia's help in the form of a being who would be a bridge for us between the stars and the Earth. Our city evolved out of the work of this group and was originally a place where we performed the invocations to invite a mountain spirit.

When this spirit came, it spread its presence over the land and drew to itself what it needed to integrate with our world. It became a mountain in appearance, because, like you, we also appreciate the beauty and majesty of mountains rising from the landscape. This form inspires us as it does you, and draws our hearts and minds upward to its peak and thus to the peaks within ourselves.

Of course, we remain well aware of its deeper nature. And as the mountain grew and developed, integrating with the land, the city grew with it.

When I go into the mountain, then, I am entering into the energy and life of one of the great servants of Gaia, one who itself can perceive the cosmic energies and draw them into our world. It holds the basic pattern of the work that I do.

Many of the spirits that form the mountains of our world are also connected to the physical mountains in your world. Mountain spirits are among humanity's greatest allies in the changes that you face, though you don't yet realize it. In my case, the spirit of my mountain is intimately associated with this work of mountain spirits in your world and, I believe, is connected to one of the great mountains where you live. This creates a further resonance between us, a point of contact between the land where I live and work and the one you inhabit. Through the mountains we share, we can find greater links between us.

This was the end of the "left-over". It actually was a fairly significant bit of information, which is why, in the midst of everything else I was receiving from Mariel, I was unable to hold on to all of this as well, though I sensed it at the time and knew I had lost something important.

Where I live is surrounded by mountains. It's one reason I wanted to live here and why I love this area. Mountains have special gifts of spirit to offer us, I feel, quite apart from any contact with the Sidhe which they may facilitate. They can be honored and appreciated just for themselves.

Nevertheless, as I thought about this message, I had a flash that Mount Rainier, the beautiful mountain that so dominates Puget Sound, was connected to the spirit of the mountain that overlooked Mariel's land. If this is correct, then indeed it does suggest some of the links that have made this contact possible.

SIDHE AND HUMANS – "CITIZEN DIPLOMACY"

Greetings!

There has always been contact between our people, the Sidhe, and yours. Sometimes it has been harmonious, sometimes conflicted, but there has always been contact. There are also, as you know, Sidhe who do not make contact with humans and have little or no wish to do so. It's impossible to make generalizations, and I would not wish you to do so.

I see in your mind your memory of the citizen diplomacy between your country and your adversary at the time, the Soviet Union. Not all of your citizens took part in this, many did not even know about it, and some would not have taken part because they deeply believed that the Soviet Union was the enemy and could not be trusted.

But there were different organizations that orchestrated this diplomatic contact between citizens and ordinary people. Sometimes they knew of each other, and sometimes they didn't, but all were responding to an ideal and to a need, which was to build bridges and foster understanding between the two peoples. Yet the background to this effort was that there was always a level of contact between the Russians and yourselves; people traveled for ordinary reasons of family, business, art, science, and curiosity between the two countries, paying little heed to the political or diplomatic tensions

It is similar for us. There is a background level of contact between your people and mine that has always been there, sometimes waxing, sometimes waning in its ebb and flow, but always there. Sometimes members of my people have made singular efforts to affect and shape human affairs, if only on local levels. So in this sense, there is nothing revolutionary about the contact we make with you now.

On the other hand, the times are different. Events happening on a planetary scale make efforts towards reconciliation important. We are entering a new time upon the planet that will affect both our peoples as never before, and there is a need for us to help each other and find again the patterns of wholeness that once we knew. With this in mind, there are now "citizen diplomats" among my people who seek to make contact with humans and develop partnership and mutual assistance.

Many of these individuals live or work closer to your plane than I do. This is why I need the assistance of my two companions to connect with you and to enter your world. There are those Sidhe farther "upstream" than I who find it very difficult to connect with you and do so through intermediaries within the subtle realms. I and my associates here are in-between. We are not on the borders, so to speak, as some of our people are, but we are not far distant in the uplands either.

My associates and I undertook a task to make the citizen diplomacy between our worlds easier, and the creation of the card deck is a tool in this regard. This class has been another experiment in building a field between us, and a successful one, we feel.

The need, you see, is for us to connect with you in your incarnate state; it is the power within your incarnation that is important to us. There is a synthesis possible between the structure of your incarnation and the structure of ours that is important to the future. We can help you be more incarnated, and you can do the same for us, but the real goal is to bring into being a new kind of incarnation—not a new kind of physical body necessarily but a new etheric and subtle structure that will serve you better in the world that is unfolding.

For example, you have built patterns and habits in your collective development that isolate you from the world around you and from the life within nature; as a result your collective incarnation is out of balance—lop-sided, you would say—which means from the world's point of view, you are less incarnated than you could be. We can help with this. We can be part of the process that brings you back into balance and restores connections with the world. We are the embodiments of the qualities that are dormant but needed within yourselves. And of course, you have much to offer us as well that arises from the depths of the incarnational work which you do. As I said, we bring starlight, the power of connection and spaciousness, but you bring fire from the depths of the earth and the depths of your incarnations.

I am most certainly not the leader of the citizen diplomacy arising from our side. In a sense, there is no single leader for this operation as it unfolds on several fronts in different ways, just as the citizen diplomacy did in your world. This is an area where we do not wish to be too explicit, for you have a habit as human beings of overly-concretizing and turning the particular into the universal. The borderland between us is fluid and needs to remain so, as free as possible from projections and expectations.

I have shared with you some of who I am and some of my life so that you would come to see me as a person and not as an abstraction, a voice of wisdom from the fabled realm of the Sidhe. I do bring a certain authority and skill to this work between us, but only in a local way. I and my associates are simply one of many groups attempting in many different ways to perform our "citizen diplomacy" with you.

While we delight in being helpful in your lives in whatever way we can, we do not come to you as guides or even as spiritual allies in the same way that you may have companions and co-workers from the subtle realms of spirit. How a particular Sidhe may interact with a particular human is entirely a function of the relationship that develops between them. It is up to the people involved. We are not setting forth an agenda or organizational protocols! Certain Sidhe for their own reasons may wish to be more involved with you and may take an interest in many parts of your life and work, and other Sidhe may not and may seem more impersonal and distant. But this is because you are working with individuals who differ in their temperaments, skills and needs, just as you do. We learn and grow with you at the same time. And while we can be helpful in many ways, we are not "superSidhe," all powerful and all knowing.

There is a common impulse to undertake this work with you that many of us feel, and we each try to make the contributions that are within our talents and skills to do so. But this is not the same as saying that we are all part of a homogenous organization that has everything planned and plotted. So the reasons you find yourselves in contact with a particular Sidhe have as much to do with you and your work as with us but also with opportunity and, as you say, resonance. There is no master Sidhe handing out assignments. We go where we are able and do what we are able.

This is enough for now. Blessings as always.

THE PRACTICE OF COLLABORATION – PART 1

Mariel's personal sharing of some of the elements of her life and work seemed to open a door in the class. As one participant wrote to me, "I was struggling with making a connection before, but Mariel's latest message makes her seem more human to me. Suddenly I get it! I get what she's about and what we're trying to do!" The whole energy of the gathering moved up a notch.

One thing that had become clear to me over the months of communicating with Mariel is how practical she and her other Sidhe companions are. They are not philosophers. They want to accomplish something. Throughout the class, I had felt Mariel struggling to "ground" her contact with us, to make it real, and to open up doors for genuine work together. Finally, with the breakthrough that her personal sharing seemed to have created, the opportunity arose to address the actual practice of collaboration.

What followed was a very long communication. It was a session that began in the afternoon of one day and continued on and off through the morning of the next day. During this time, I would move in and out of contact with her, and I imagine I was busy that night while I was sleeping, too, though my sleep was dreamless. By the time I had sorted out and put into words all that Mariel was trying to communicate while taking advantage of the energy that had opened up for her, I was ready for a break!

For convenience, I've broken up this long communication into four parts.

Greetings! The practical questions are important—they are key to our working together. What may we give to you, and how? What may you give to us, and how? What are the realistic dimensions of our collaboration? How may we proceed?

Remember that the answers may vary from person to person since each relationship is unique, just as is true with your own friendships with other humans. How you may relate to one person and what you do together may be very different from how you relate to and what you do with someone else. The specific nature of our engagement with any one of you depends on who you are as well as who we are, on the circumstances involved, and even on factors that influence the tides of energy that flow between your world and mine.

Let us begin with what we need from you.

We need a deeper understanding of who you are in your world, as well as of the world you have created. When you attune to us, giving us access to your thoughts and allowing us to participate in your world with you, we gain insights we would not have otherwise. This helps us in our work, too.

Remember that the reconciliation between human and Sidhe is part of a much larger project of integration going on in the world as a whole as Gaia moves to establish a greater coherency within herself. We contribute to this, as do many others. Frankly, the human world is both a driver of this integration and one of its obstacles. Knowing how to understand and work with your energies and your world—and to have a better attunement to ordinary humanity—is an important asset to those of us working with this project.

We need to understand your connection to matter, the love you bring to it and the love you draw out from it. This is something even you do not always understand or think much about. You take your physicality for granted, not always realizing the miracles embedded within it.

Further, as I have said, when we do approach your world, for many of us it is as if we become "wispy". Attunement to your solidity and your connection to matter helps us maintain our solidity of purpose and presence as well.

To do our work, we need your help in drawing close to your world. But for many of us, your world is filled with turbulent and often painful energies. We need your help in buffering the impacts that arise from the conflicts you experience and create. This is so whether the conflicts are physical or psychological. I am not speaking here of your personal emotional conflicts; these we can weather if need be and may even be able to help. Instead, it is the impact of your collective negativity that makes it hard for us to approach. We need your help in bypassing this, like you would build a road around a swamp. You do this by finding your own calm and peace in the midst of your life. If you stand in serenity, we can stand there with you.

We are deeply attuned to harmony, joy and peace. We are, after all, by your designation the People of Peace. If with your help, we can stand in the energies of your world, then we can be a presence of peace upon which you may draw in your efforts to create peace.

You have an experience of the Sacred and of life different from our own, one born of the challenges and sufferings you face as physical beings. As I said earlier, the diamonds of sacredness are everywhere to be found, but when you must dig for them, they carry with them the power of the effort. We would like to be invited to share the fire of your sacredness.

In effect, you know the Sacred in ways we do not, and I daresay the reverse is also true. You have inner pathways into the Light that are new and strange to us, and we would learn to walk those paths with you.

Beyond this, there may be specific tasks or objectives around which we can collaborate, projects arising both from our end and from yours. What these may be, we cannot say. Some of you already engage with us in your teaching work or in healing. Some of you undertake work that has no correspondence in our world, or very little, and when invited to participate, we are fascinated and informed by what we see and experience, though we may not know at first how or what to contribute. As I said, we enjoy being introduced to your world.

In summary, we need to build bridges to your world in order to more effectively offer the gifts we possess. In your attunement to us, you help these bridges to form.

THE PRACTICE OF COLLABORTION – PART 2

And now the how. How do you do build these bridges?

Certainly, casual and friendly contact is possible. Remember that we are telepathic and empathic beings attuned to patterns of subtle energies. So we can be aware of your thoughts and feelings and of the energies that surround you. These communicate to us. If you hold us in your thoughts and invite us into your world, we can be aware of this and can respond if conditions permit it. This is particularly true if there is already some link of familiarity between us. If we know you, we can find you.

However, to work together, it's beneficial if a more stable and integrated connection is created. How may this be done?

I wish to elaborate upon what I said earlier about how we make contact with your world. Imagine that you are stepping into a fast moving stream. Maintaining your balance is difficult. The current may cause you to fall, sweeping you away from where you wish to be. Even if this does not happen, it takes energy to move against the current and stay in balance. This can be tiring and draining, limiting the time you can stay in the stream. However, if there are stones in the stream upon which you can stand, then you are better able to maintain your footing and balance and moving in the stream is easier, requiring less energy.

Your world, so solid to you, is like this stream to us. But there are stones we can stand on. Some are there naturally, places in the world that possess affinity with us. Some we can create with the help of nature spirits and the beings of Faerie. Our affinity with life enables us to reach into the natural world and weave support structures of energy that provide the "rocks" upon which we can stand. And you can be stones for us.

I should say that the reverse is also true: that when you enter our world or any subtle world, you can find yourself in a swift-moving stream. What are the rocks on which you stand so you are not swept away? The objectives and the principles are the same whether we are coming from our end or you are coming from yours. We share a common problem, which is to maintain the stability that allows an effective connection and partnership to be formed.

Affinity is a key. Originally the "standing stones" in the circles that formed portals between our worlds and created the "rocks" upon which we could stand were individuals, both Sidhe and human. These were persons with deep affinity for life and for the world around them. They were so connected to themselves, to the world, and to the forces of life that they created around themselves a field of stability and peace rooted in the earth. When such individuals combined their energies, this field expanded, creating a "middle-earth" that was neither wholly physical nor wholly subtle, neither wholly human nor wholly Sidhe or Faerie.

In time, as you know, these individuals became replaced by actual stones which performed much the same function, though with decreasing effectiveness as time passed.

Though I have referred to such places as portals between our world and yours, they are not really doorways as such. We can open the pathways between our worlds anywhere and anytime we wish, but as I say, such pathways may lead us into streams where there are no rocks on which to stand and find stability. These circles created large stones, so to speak, where the stream of earthly and human energies flowed around them, forming a stable space for us to enter.

I tell you this story so you can see that the true stone circle is an inner condition of consciousness, affinity and connectedness. Because of this, you can create stones in the river for us as well, and we can work with you in this process, thereby fashioning a bridge that allows us to cross the rapids without being swept away. The more you practice this, the more stable and powerful the "stone" within and around you becomes, which can have value for you in your own life quite apart from being a condition of connectedness with us.

While we can form connections of resonance with you improvisationally in the moment, based on familiarity and the flow of energy between us, the building of these stones of connection takes time and is a deliberate process. To facilitate this, we provided you with the cards which can stimulate—and simulate—the power of the stone circle within you.

So you can begin with the cards. However you use them, make them your ally in beginning to connect with us. They are designed to replicate the ancient circles and the stability they created that made them portals and stepping stones for our mutual use. Therefore, we suggest that if you wish to deepen your connection with us, you use the cards in a regular way—in whatever manner seems best and natural to you—to build what you call the felt sense of the Stone Circle within yourself. Come to know yourself as a walking Stone Circle, carrying its stability and connectedness wherever you go in your life. This will also alert and awaken you to our presence and the bond between us. Remember that we connect to you as individuals, so what one person may experience is not necessarily what another person will.

In this process, do not use the cards for oracular purposes. This introduces a whole other element and puts you more in touch with the subtle realms than with us. You can perform divination with the cards at any time, but for this particular work of building the stones in the stream, use the cards exclusively for attunement to the stone circle and to us.

However, you should see the cards as a starting point, not as an ending or as important in themselves. They bring the presence of the stone circles into your life, but remember, the original standing stones were individuals. So in a sense, the purpose of the cards is to take you back in time to before the stones themselves were erected. It is even to make the cards themselves unnecessary in your life, at least for this purpose. We wish you to internalize the stone circle so that you become alive to your own affinities to life, your own wholeness, your own stability, your own rootedness in the earth, your own dancing and joyous nature. Never forget that *you* are the portal, *you* are the stepping stone in the river, *you* are the presence of peace and integration with whom we may connect in stable partnership.

Therefore, anything you do in your life, any practice you undertake, that enhances your sense of connection with the world and with life, that expands your lovingness and joy, that attunes you to a center of peace and wonder within you, will strengthen your standing as a "stone" of stability and wholeness that we can use.

THE PRACTICE OF COLLABORATION - PART 3

Our overall desire is for you to be yourselves and to know yourselves as beings of joy and peace, love and wisdom, filled with magic and miracles. In you, stars and earth meet, and the wonder of that meeting is still unfolding its potentials. We wish above all for you to honor who you are for as you do so, you cannot help but honor the life that is around you, including ourselves.

In partnership with us, our desire is for you to become like the Old Ones who stood and formed the first circles. You can do this, you know. It is in you as fully as it is in us. Of course, times have changed since those ancient days, and the needs of the world are different. The condition of the world is different, too, and humanity itself has changed. You are less child-like than you were then. In some ways you have become darker, but in other ways you shine more brightly and carry a hard-won wisdom and connection to the world. Paradoxically, though we have and have always had a deep affinity for nature and for life, through you we can discover a deeper connection with the world, for you are in touch with the life within matter in ways we are not. If you will listen, it speaks to you with voices we do not hear. We know the voices of starlight but you hear the voices of the fire within earth and matter.

So, in addition to the cards as tools of attunement to us, I suggest that you take time to build upon your attunements to the matter that is around you. Attune to life in all its forms, whether that of creature or artifact. I suggest you take time to attune to the sacredness within you that can connect you to the sacredness within the substance of the world. And I suggest you take time to attune to your own self and to the soul that grows within you. While none of these things are directly related to us, such attunements make you a better "stone", able to stand in your world with power and stability, integrated and connected. Then when you turn to us, you do so as a living portal, a living stepping stone allowing us to stand in the river with you and not be swept away.

You have asked if we can see through your eyes, hear through your ears as you go about your daily activities. The answer is not always and not necessarily as clearly as we would like. We can be present to you, drawn by the links between us that you are forging, but we may not have clear access to your experiences even though we can see to some extent the state of your thoughts and feelings.

As in all things dealing with the translation of experience from one dimension to another, much depends on the quality and stability of energy at the point of contact. To use my metaphor, if you are a standing stone, we can more easily touch you and see what you see; if, however, you are a wavering reed bending in the wind or a leaf floating and bobbing on the rushing stream, it is harder for us to connect and maintain a clear focus. This is why casual contact may give a sense of our presence but not fulfill the conditions for a strong sharing of experience.

If, however, you have made a practice of attunement to your own stable center and of attunement to us, then you stand strongly in your own presence, and we can connect.

Here is an image I see in David's mind, more modern than my images of stones and rivers. Think of trying to hear a radio station in the midst of static when the signal wavers and loses its focus. You catch a word here and there but the overall message is garbled. But if the signal is stable and your radio can find it amidst all the other signals, then the message is clear.

We can readily feel and appreciate your desire for us, your love for us, your willingness to incorporate us into your lives. But this is just the beginning. It is a foundation upon which a more solid and stable structure of contact can be built. You need to do the work and the practice, just as we do.

I have spoken of my altar that I dedicate to my human contacts. It is often with me in my thoughts, but I also spend time each day in attunement to it, to you and to your world. I cannot take our contact for granted. I must do my work as well. And part of the doing of it is to discover my own humanity, the part of me that most connects to who you are and who we are together in our deepest shared identity.

You can use the cards to attune to us, as I have said. You can use the glyph that my colleagues have provided. You can use other means that are resonant with you as an individual: a stone, a tree, a place in nature, a bowl of water, a candle flame, whatever gives you a sense of connection to our world. What you use is not as important as that you practice the attunement and internalize what you experience as you connect with your own "Sidhe-ness", the part of you that most connects to who we are and who we are together in our deepest shared identity.

Invite us into your life when you are feeling joy and the beauty of the world. Invite us into your life when you are undertaking your daily tasks. Invite us into your world when sorrow overtakes you and you feel the weight of compassion within your heart. Invite us into your presence when you honor and celebrate the presence of sacredness, for we would know the Sacred that you experience.

If you invite us from the place where you are a standing stone, the connection will be easier for us both and more will be exchanged.

THE PRACTICE OF COLLABORATION - PART 4

What may we bring to you?

We bring you partnership in endeavors to help Gaia unfold her potentials.

We bring you the remembrance of who you are and of your

ancient self at one with life, at one with the world. We bring you our vision of who you are and can be.

We bring you remembrance of the existence of magic. Our magic is not yours, but this does not mean you are not equally magical or that you don't have your own magic. Your magic arises from your humanity and the way you embody yourself in the world. It is there for you to discover, but only if you stop projecting the reality of magic outside yourself and onto others in other realms. Yes, the realm of Faerie has magic. Yes, we have magic. But our magic grows organically out of who we are and out of our connections with our world. You have your connections, your identity, your magical nature as well. You hold wonder within you as fully as we hold it in ourselves. If we remind you of its existence, perhaps then you can find your way into its reality within you.

Remember that we are not subtle beings nor beings of spirit. There are things that your subtle allies can do on your behalf or with you that are not possible for us. The distinction is important, for you should not see us as "guides" or spirit allies. We would not raise expectations that we cannot meet.

Having said this, however, it does not mean that we cannot help as friends may help one another. We are masters of connection, so we can bring our skill and energies in this area into your lives to assist you as you make your own connections with the world. Think of what we offer as an enzyme or catalyst that makes connection easier and faster. You still must make the effort, but we can facilitate the process.

We bring you friendship and the love that cousins have for each other.

Beyond this, who knows? We are exploring as much as you are. Who knows what the limits or dimensions of our partnership may be?

This has been a long discourse. It is enough for now. Blessings as always.

SHARING SHOES

Greetings!

While we are not subtle beings as you understand them, we nevertheless exist at a different wavelength of energy and substance than you. Whenever this condition exists, whether with a subtle being or with one of us—or with beings equivalent to us—it is entirely possible for two individuals to be side by side and remain unaware of each other.

So what enables contact? What enables consciousness to bring the wavelengths together, or to rise out of one's groove and enter into that of another?

It is true that subtle perception can do this, but not everyone has such perceptions. Fortunately, there are other ways as well. The two which we are exploring with you are presence and resonance.

Resonance is an affinity that draws us together. Like all affinities, it is based in love but also in an act of will grounded in understanding. You have a saying about standing and walking in another's shoes. This creates affinity.

You already have some knowledge of our "shoes". We are joyous. We are attuned to peace. We are attuned to life. We have a delight for nature and for all living, growing things. We foster and nurture potentials. We are attuned to wholeness and to the connections from which it springs. We are attuned to music, dance, and creativity. We draw upon the stars as well as the earth.

This is not the whole description of who we are, but it is a start. These are the qualities—the shoes—most available to you, the easiest for you to slip into. When you think of us in a deliberate way and take on the qualities which we value, you start to walk in our shoes. There is affinity. There is resonance. You can feel how we invite you into our lives, and as you respond, you will discover more about the shoes, more about who we are.

Likewise, by engaging with you, we come to understand your shoes so we can put them on as well. This is one of the gifts you offer us by inviting us into your lives. It's a gift that enhances and expands, for as we come to know you, we can form a deeper affinity and resonance.

I have said that I have an altar that I dedicate to our contact. This is not an altar for worship, you understand. It is a place—a condition—in which I may attune to you and discover how to form affinity with you. It is a place in which I hold the qualities that make up your lives, your "shoes".

The second tool is presence. The more solidly you are yourself, the more attuned you are to your own being, your own presence, the more you stand out. Presence crosses wavelengths and is not bound by them.

In this regard, your work with the stone circle represented by the cards can lead you to this presence. Stones have great presence and they can augment your own. Think of the circle like a lens that brings things into clearer, shaper focus. When you stand in the center of the circle, surrounded by the Stones, by the spirit of the Old Ones, you are the focal point of this lens. Feel the power of the circle bringing you into greater focus, greater clarity, greater presence. In this way, the stone circle serves to foster you and heightens your felt sense of identity and presence. You can carry this felt sense into affinity with us.

We are skilled in telepathy and empathy. Even if we are on different wavelengths, with affinity, resonance and presence, our minds and hearts come into contact, and you can feel what we think, think what we feel, and know we are with you energetically even if you cannot "see" us on our wavelength. Let your mind's eye and your heart's eye do your seeing and your hearing.

If you dedicate, as I have done, some part of your environment to be an altar to our contact, then the energies of affinity, resonance, and presence can be grounded and enhanced by something concrete in your life; such a place or thing can be an ally between us.

However, remember, you are the stone circle. You carry within you at all times the means to stand in presence, stand in affinity, open in resonance, and thus reach across the wavelengths to those of us who are reaching back.

Blessings!

A FINAL MESSAGE AT CLASS'S ENDING

Greetings!

These final thoughts I would share with you. What we most wish in our engagement with you is to enable you to be more fully yourself, more fully human. For the fullness of your humanity includes what we are as the Sidhe. Just as there are stars within the earth and sometimes the way to go up is to go down, so the deep path into the Sidhe runs through yourself and who you are. Find your way to us through your own being.

This is true for us as well, for the fullness of being Sidhe also lies along a path that leads through what you are and are becoming. The path of the human leads us more deeply into the Sidhe. The path of the Sidhe leads you more deeply into the human.

So do not seek us out in ways that would diminish yourself or your humanity. Stand proudly in who you are and you will be able to stand with us. We do not come to you ashamed or needful in our Sidhe-ness; we come in our power and presence. How else may you be aware of us? How else may we offer our gifts to you? Do the same. Come to us in the fullness of your Light and presence, aware of your gifts, your presence; then we can be aware of you. Then we can be partners.

Remember, we are skilled in connection and thus in manifestation. We cannot undertake your tasks for you or solve the problems that you face. You must formulate your way through your own understanding and will. But once you do, once you set forth your intent, we can blend with the field you create and enhance its capacities to connect and to manifest. We cannot do what a human being can and must do, but we can accompany you, partner you, and enhance you as you do these things. Our fields of energy can sing together and thus draw more from the world as it seeks to manifest your intent.

So do not turn to us to do it for you, whatever it may be. But stand in your power and presence, and we can stand with you and do it with you .

In this partnership, be aware that we may ask help of you and of the energies you can invoke. In our work to assist the powers of nature, human energies and human blessings can be a powerful asset. Just be aware that telepathically, intuitively, or through synchronicity, you may know our call for help should it come. It may be subtle, it may be faint, but it will be there. Be alert to when it happens.

I and my colleagues thank you for your willingness to participate in this gathering. You have provided us with a chance to know you better and to enhance the foundations on which we both may stand to give blessings to the earth.

Blessings!

FINAL THOUGHTS

Before ending this part of the book, I wanted to share some of my impressions in working with Mariel and receiving her thoughts (and being her amanuensis) through the duration of the class. It was the most sustained contact that I've had with them; in one form or another, there was contact every day for the six weeks that we all met together online. This gave me some interesting insights both into the Sidhe and into myself in relationship to them.

One thing that came across strongly as the days passed was that Mariel and her companions began to feel like Indigenous people to me. In their attunement to nature and the earth, in their sense of wholeness and connectedness, and in their awareness of the life within all things and the wonderment of that life, they reminded me of native peoples whom I've met. Evidently they possess a highly developed civilization, with its own form of technology, but it's a civilization very different from our own. From what Mariel has shown me, their cities are profoundly integrated with the countryside. Everyone, wherever they live, feels part of the land and draws life from it and gives back to it. The Earth is Mother in much the way that it is for so many indigenous peoples in our world.

The other thing is that there is a quality about Mariel and about all the Sidhe that I've met that I can only translate as *wild* or *untamed*. It's a quality that I've felt when I've been hiking in deep woods out in wilderness. It's a world governed by different rules and laws than those that I'm used to in the city or in the suburb where I live.

Mariel comes across to me as a highly civilized, highly trained and cultured individual, yet at the same time, there is something fierce about her. There is a power in her and around her that can't be constrained or defined by human norms and expectations.

Years ago, I was at a party at a friend's house. One of the people attending was a woman who brought her animal companion with her. At first it seemed like a large dog, but I soon learned that it was more wolf than dog. My friend had a sunken living room such that when you were seated on the sofa, your head was actually level with the surrounding floor. At one point in the evening, I felt this powerful presence behind me. Turning my head, I found myself looking directly into the eyes of this magnificent animal who was lying on the floor just behind me, its head level with mine I'll never forget the intelligence in those eyes and the sense of wildness about it.

The sense I had with this wolf-dog is akin to the sense I often have of Mariel. It reminds me that while she is gracious and loving and can look very human—at least when she has a shape I can see—she's not human at all and in some ways not definable in human terms

I bring this up because it became an issue during the class for me. As the days passed, I could tell that Mariel was working hard, in her words, to "put on her human shoes." She was making an effort to be as human-like as possible. I discovered that this lulled me into a false sense that she was in fact a disembodied human woman. I realized that I was contributing to her taking on more of a human face by the thought-forms that I was creating about her. In one way this was helpful, but in another, it got in the way.

This came home to me part way through the class when I realized that I was in danger of losing contact with her because I was attuning to my human images of Mariel rather than to Mariel herself. She wished to humanize herself in order to make contact easier, but this process couldn't go too far lest the distinctive Sidhe qualities be lost. We might be "cousins" and have a shared ancient ancestor, but in the millennia that have passed, we have become two different people, and there is strength and creativity in that difference.

So from then on, every time I made contact with her, I made an extra effort to go past the familiarity that was building up between us, as useful as that familiarity was, and to attune to the wildness that I had felt with her originally when we first made contact. I knew if I wanted to hear her accurately, I needed to attune to who she is, not who I might think she is.

BRINGING IT HOME

My concern in the class was that it not simply be a venue for sharing messages from Mariel but also a place to learn and to share about how to use the teachings and presence of the Sidhe in practical ways in our own lives. I needn't have worried. While everyone appreciated and benefited from what she had to say, the participants were all willing and able to share their own insights and stories of experiences with the Sidhe. Some of the stories were amazing and moving. It was evident that for a number of the participants, the Sidhe—or beings like the Sidhe—were important partners in their lives.

In order to create a safe climate in my classes so that people feel free to share openly, we all sign a Covenant of Confidentiality that nothing that anyone says will be shared outside the class without that person's permission. Like Las Vegas, what happens in a Lorian class stays in the Lorian class.

One of the participants, Søren Hauge, is a Danish spiritual teacher, counselor, and author, as well as a friend of many years. He has had contact with the Sidhe for some time, teaches workshops on how we may partner with them, and, like John Matthews, is also the author of a book on the Sidhe. He not only shared some of the communications that he had with the Sidhe, but he also shared how he integrated these "cousins" into his life and work. His comments seemed to sum up what many people experienced and felt, though each in his or her own way. With his permission, I wanted to close this chapter on the class with his comments and with a message from his contact.

"The realization that I was having Sidhe contact came gradually and finally matured into a conscious awareness of a shared presence. I have mostly experienced it as a male individual, an inner companion permeated with an atmosphere of a rocklike calmness and a poetic fluidity. Very early the name Fjeldur came to me and I realized that it was a kind of human name resembling the quality of "a mountain full of music". He has mostly supported me by his presence or a shared field where inspiration has arisen. Although I am also aware of other Sidhe, including female presences, he has been the 'door-opener' to me.

"My experience of him has been a silent, calm presence, erect and tall, with a flowing, waving, inner mobility, like long hair, blowing in the wind. It is a very close, almost physical experience, as if the smell of earth and flowers is present, and I feel a mixture of universality and a touch of Scandinavian flavor—as if he is related to the Nordic region, and at the same time free of locality.

"When I attune to him or the Sidhe in general, I always start by affirming my inner 'standing-in-being', and from there I open to the organic connectedness of nature. Sometimes I do it in my home, and often I experience it when I am in open nature, usually finding a place to sit and connect with the wind, the smells, the trees and grass, animals and birds and the nurturing Earth. Through this inner, organic intimacy there comes a fluidity and a poetic lightness, like gentle, musical variations. Images and words come very easy in this fertile flow. When it deepens, I sense a shared standing in blended movement and heart and mind are together. It is as if the wisdom that opens is tapped from nature, but it is via the kindred presence. The usual compactness of my human planning and structuring is loosened and 'in-between' the usual focal points there is a lightness, branching and flowing out, weaving and blending, making space for the creative, imaginative within me. It has a magical touch, like innocent gentleness. In my psycho-spiritual work with clients, I have experienced a sudden presence of this nature, supporting the work when I facilitate that inner, subconscious parts are transformed into greater light. At a deep level I experience that the Sidhe help me especially when I trust situations and "let go" and allow the free flow to enter with playfulness.

"An inspiration from Fjeldur can illustrate the communication emerging from the shared presence:

"We stand in our being, tall as pillars, perceiving your dignity, seeing your beauty. We are different and yet so related. From the realm of spirit, with a view to Stars, connected with the inner light of the Sacred Earth, we wish to remind us about our shared nobleness. Be always erect like stones of majesty, connecting Heaven and Earth. Let us be upstanding, elevated in honoring our Sacredness. Let us stand together so we can dance together. The blowing Winds of Spirit is the music uniting us. We can sing together, create together, in new ways – when we come together. We can bring the living streams as waving notes, dancing in and out, connecting everything. You can bring the depth and strength of rootedness, anchoring spirit in matter. In fellowship we can create a dignified partnership guarding the Earth, the domain of the Mother who brings birth to the Child of the new reality, the song of tenderness, the new world of Creation."

PART III

THE EXERCISES

INTRODUCTION

When working with my subtle world colleagues in a class setting, it is not unusual for them to suggest an exercise or practice for the class participants to try out. Mariel had done so as well in the past, the prime example being the Guardian Mantle exercise. However, for some reason, I was not expecting them to do so in the Sidhe class, so I was surprised when Mariel, as part of one of her conversations with me, presented a series of exercises around the theme of attuning to stellar energies.

Jeremy and I presented other exercises in the class as well, centered around the *Card Deck of the Sidhe* and specific ways of using the cards for attunement and meditation. Because this is not a book about the card deck itself, I've only included one or two of those exercises here. If you are interested in pursuing them, the information may be found in the "Card Deck" section of the Library on the Lorian Website, under "Card Essays".

ATTUNEMENT TO THE SIDHE

There are probably as many ways to attune to the Sidhe as there are individual humans and individual Sidhe since ultimately attunement is a matter of resonance between the hearts and minds of individuals. In my own case, my attunement to the Sidhe was initiated from their end. Once the contact was made, I had their "address", so to speak, written in the felt sense of their energy within my body and my mind. I could then attempt to contact them by attuning to that felt sense. However, since I didn't seek them out in the first place, I didn't have an experience of making contact with them "from scratch".

Over the years, I've talked with Mariel about this. Her position has been that attunement and contact with the Sidhe is not a technique as much as it is a mindset. At the very least it entails accepting their existence and that there can be a bond between us. Once she said to me:

When you attune to nature, you bring yourself close to us. When you attune to the stars, you bring yourself close to us. When you attune to joy and wonder, you touch the fabric of our realm. When you touch your own sacredness, you touch the bond we share. Think of us when you do these things, and you may find a bridge opening between us.

In the weeks preceding the class, this matter of how to teach attunement and partnership with the Sidhe was much on my mind. After all, it was a class on the Sidhe. I felt I wanted to offer practical information that people could take away with them when it was over. What role did the Sidhe play? How to contact them in the first place? I began to fret about this. Finally, Mariel said:

> You wonder what to do with us. You question, How do we fit into your lives—or you into ours? I understand. You are an explorer and a teacher; you seek information and understanding that you can pass on to others. But be careful not to over think this. Don't worry so much! Find a space for us in your hearts, and we will work out the details of how to connect with your lives and what to do when the connection is made. We have much to offer, I feel, but we are exploring as well what is possible and what is not. We do not always know what we can contribute or the form that it may take. We break new territory together! The agendas will be shaped as the relationship evolves. Again I say, don't wonder or worry overmuch. Just be yourself, and we will be ourselves, and we'll see what evolves. What is important is that we make space for each other.

When I wrote the manual for the *Card Deck of the Sidhe*, I included some specific exercises for attuning to the Sidhe using the cards as meditative tools. Likewise, in his book, *The Sidhe*, John Matthews describes an exercise he was given by his Sidhe contact using a specific symbol or glyph as a meditative focal point. I was hoping that Mariel might do something similar in the class.

However, as I've mentioned, her interest was less on having us attune to her or her companions and more on our attuning to our own sacredness and to the Sidhe-qualities within us. "The more you attune to your inner legacy," she said, "the more you come into resonance with us." Consequently, the exercises she did give had this as theme.

Most of these exercises focused around the stars and attuning to stellar energies. Mariel often referred to both humans and Sidhe as having "star souls" and that our deepest link could be found in a mutual attunement to this part of ourselves. As she said, the stars weren't simply points of light in the sky but the realm of cosmic intelligence and Light, filled with forces able to balance and harmonize our earthy and planetary natures. The germ of these forces were innate in each of us as a kind of "inner star self", and the attunement to the stars was in fact an attunement to this aspect of our nature. As we did so, Mariel felt we would naturally and organically open pathways between us.

There is another reason. When I attune to the stars, what I feel is the spaciousness of the universe. When I take that spaciousness into myself, I can feel the spirit of new potentials coming alive. There is wonder there, not only the wonder of the cosmos itself but the wonder of our own creative imagination and beingness. Space has sometimes been called the "next frontier", but this isn't true. We are the next frontier as we seek to explore new realms and possibilities of connectedness, wholeness, love, and even magic. The Sidhe wish to explore these realms and possibilities with us. Through the spaciousness of our "star-selves" and theirs, we find the partnership that can make this exploration a joyous adventure.

Here are the star exercises Mariel offered.

ATTUNEMENT TO STELLAR ENERGIES

Exercise 1: Standing in the Night

The simplest and more straightforward exercise Mariel suggested is simply to go outside at night and be in the presence of the stars. Nothing quite substitutes for the actual physical encounter with the night sky. Feel the starlight falling on the earth and plants around you. Feel it on yourself. Pay attention to any sensations, images, thoughts, feelings you may have in the presence of the stars.

Then feel yourself expanding into the vastness of the cosmos, becoming more spacious within yourself as you commune with the stars. If you wish, feel a space opening up in you in which the stars may enter and shine as you hold the heavens within yourself. What does this feel like?

(If you live in a city, light pollution may make it hard to see the stars at night and thus diminish the effect of this exercise. If possible, find a way to go where it is darker and you can see the stars.)

Exercise 2: A Star Visits

This exercise is a variant of the preceding one.

- Stand under the stars in the night sky

- Turn your attention to a single star of your choice

- Imagine this star becoming brighter. Greet it with love and appreciation.

- Imagine a beam of starlight coming from this star and striking the earth in front of you. Where it does so, it turns into a being made of starlight.

- Welcome and bless this being and ask that it help you feel and know your own inner star-being, the star-Light within your own body and soul. The object here is communion, not receiving a message. The object is to allow this being to reawaken within you your sense of kinship and resonance with stellar energies.

- When the visit seems complete, the star-visitor dissolves back into starlight and returns to its source. Send it on its way with appreciation and love.

Note: When Mariel presented this exercise, I couldn't help but think of two of my favorite movies, *Stardust* and the third Narnia movie, *Voyage of the Dawn Treader*. In both of these movies, a star comes to earth and turns into a person.

Exercise 3: Drawing on Star Stuff

Science tells us that we are all made of "star-stuff" as the elements in our bodies were all created in the heart of stars and then released into the universe when the stars went nova. You can do this exercise either outside or inside, but I think standing outside in nature provides a greater richness.

- Standing or sitting outside or inside, observe and contemplate the things around you. Everything you see is composed of atoms that once were brought into being within the depths of stars. Thus, within all things is a deep memory of being part of a star.

- Attune to something in your environment that is a mineral. It could be a stone, a brick wall, the pavement under your feet. Invite the atoms of this object to remember their origin in the stars. Feel the presence of this star-stuff within this object.

- From this star-stuff, draw a thread of starlight from the object into your self, where it joins with the star-stuff in your own body, the memory of your own atoms of their stellar past.

- Attune to a plant in your environment. Invite the atoms within this plant to remember their origin in the stars. Feel the presence of this star-stuff within the plant.

- From this star-stuff, draw a thread of starlight from the plant into your self, where it joins with the star-stuff in your own body, the memory of your own atoms of their stellar past.

- If there are animals or birds in your environment, attune to one of them as well. Invite the atoms within this creature to remember their origin in the stars. Feel the presence of this star-stuff within the animal or bird.

- From this star-stuff, draw a thread of starlight from the creature into your self, where it joins with the star-stuff in your own body, the memory of your own atoms of their stellar past.

- Feel star-stuff everywhere in the world around you, its ancient star-light linking you and the world with the stars in the cosmos. What is the felt sense of this? Feel yourself as mobile, thinking, aspiring star-stuff given form, living and acting in a world made just as you are from the bodies of stars. What is the felt sense of this?

- Allow this sense of the star-stuff within you and within all things to attune you to your own stellar elements, the star-parts of you that blend and merge with the elements of the earth.

Exercise 4: Home Star

This exercise is based on the fact that the sun is a star: our home star.

- Begin this exercise by standing or sitting outside in sunlight.

- Feel the sunlight bathing everything in the environment around you. Feel the sunlight on yourself.

- Close your eyes and imagine a golden river of sunlight flowing between you and the sun. Release yourself to this river and feel it drawing you into the golden orb of the sun.

- As you enter the presence of the sun, you become aware that at its heart is the consciousness of a star, a member of a cosmic community of stars. The golden river you are in likewise changes into a silvery river of starlight that passes into the heart of the sun, your home star, and then flows out in countless directions as many rivers, linking this star with the stars of the heavens around it.

- Rest for as long as feels comfortable in the heart of the sun, embraced by its solar energies and love but at the same time aware of the starlight that is also part of this home star, starlight that also embraces you and touches the star-light within your own self. Ask the sun to introduce you to your own star-self.

- When you feel complete or you feel tired or restless, return to earth along the ray of solar energy, becoming gracefully and in wholeness part of your own body again, basking in the sunlight.

Exercise 5: Eating Starlight

This is another exercise using the sun as our closest star as a way of attuning to the elements of our own inner star self. This exercise requires some preparation. You should be sitting or standing where you can see the sunlight and if possible, feel it upon yourself. You should also have a green plant or plants nearby and you should have a bowl of greens, such as a salad, that you can eat.

- Feel the sunlight falling upon you and upon everything around you. We call this energy and light sunlight, but it comes from the star closes to us, so it could also be called starlight.

- Observe this sun/starlight falling upon a green plant. The chlorophyll within the leaves of this plant are taking this solar/stellar energy and turning it into physical matter.

- Take your salad or bowl of greens. Eat some of the green leaves. As you do, you are taking concretized starlight into your body, starlight transformed by the plant into physical substance.

- As you eat this green, solid starlight, it becomes part of your body where your own digestive system will transform it yet again into your own flesh. You are eating starlight and making it part of you. In each of your cells, the energy that was part of a star—our sun—is now part of you, where it joins with the stellar energies that are naturally part of who you are. Feel the starlight you eat awakening and attuning you to the starlight inherent in your own body and soul.

Exercise 6: The River's Source

The previous exercises all dealt with the physical environment, physical objects, and material sunlight and starlight. The following exercises take us into the imaginal world.

- Imagine shrinking in size and stepping into your body. Before you is a river of blood, your blood, flowing through your veins and arteries.

- Step into the river. It is warm and welcoming for it carries your life. No longer simply a flow of circulation, the river you are in is now the mythic river of blood. To your left, it flows downstream towards your distant future, carrying life into your as-yet-unrealized potentials. To your right, it flows from the highlands of your ancient past.

- Turn to your right and begin wading upstream through the river of blood. As you do so, you occasionally see sparkles of silvery light in the river. These are pieces of starlight.

- As you move upstream, you are moving through time, and in this magical, mythical place, you move quickly. As you do, the number of silvery sparkles increases.

- You begin to see that the nature of the river is changing. As you near its source, its color is changing from red to silver. You realize you are increasingly stepping through starlight rather than blood.

- The source of the river is a bright Light, a spacious presence. As you approach it, you realize the blood is now totally a river of starlight and stellar energy. Then, when you are ready, you step into the river's source, into the stellar presence that is your beginning as well. What is this like? What is the felt sense of this?

- Stay in this presence as long as feels comfortable. When you are ready, step back into the river, a river of starlight, and begin moving downstream, carrying with you a felt sense of attunement to your own stellar source.

- As you move downstream, starlight turns back into blood, yet you can sense within it is an invisible stream, a river of starlight always present, always part of you.

- When the river has completely turned back to blood, you find yourself back in your body. Step out of the river and into your body, filling it completely with grace and balance, carrying with you the attunement to the river of stars within you.

Exercise 7: Star Blood

- Imagine shrinking in size and stepping into your body. Before you is a river of blood, your blood, flowing through your veins and arteries. Step into this river, which is warm and welcoming as it carries your life throughout your body.

- As you stand in this river, you become aware of another river running parallel to the one you are in. It is a river of silvery light.

- Step out of the river of your blood and into the river of silvery light. As you do, you realize it is a river of star-blood, flowing from the life of vast stellar beings. Standing in it, you can feel it flowing through the life of the sun and from there into the life of Gaia, the world soul. Star blood flows through everything in your world. It flows through you, and now you are standing in this flow.

- Take however long you wish to stand in this flowing river of star light and star blood. What does it feel like?

- When you feel complete, step out of this flowing, silvery river and back into the river of your own life, your own blood. Feel its warmth and its earth-light. Feel flowing within it your own life-light.

- Step out of this river of blood and into the fullness of your body, carrying with you grace and balance and an attunement to the two rivers within you.

Further Exercises

Exercise 8: Using the Sidhe Cards

The last three exercises use the *Card Deck of the Sidhe*. There is a power in the deck, but these exercises can certainly be done simply using your imaginations, as the cards are mainly used as visual aids and meditative prompts.

In this exercise, if you have a copy of the *Card Deck of the Sidhe*, find and take out the following five cards: The Gate of Stars, the Howe, the Stag and Pool, the Altar, and the Edge. You are going to form an L shape with them as shown below. You will be moving inward in contemplation with the first three cards and then outward into yourself and the world with the last two cards.

If you don't have a copy of the card deck, then read through the exercise to gain a sense of its objective and how the cards are being used. You can then imagine and intuit the same process.

Arrange these cards in a deck face-down so that the Edge is on the bottom, followed in order by the Altar, the Stag and Pool, the Howe, and the Gate of Stars. In this way, as you draw them, you will draw the Gate of Stars first and the Edge last.

- Draw the Gate of Stars and lay it down on the table. This is your portal to the stars. Through this Gate, the stellar energies flow into your life. Contemplate this and feel into this flow.

- Draw the Howe and lay it down on the table under the Gate of Stars. The stellar energies are now drawn into your interior. Contemplate this. You are the Howe, with stars above you and within you.

- Draw the Stag and Pool and lay it down on the table under the Howe. Within you is an ancient pool of energy and life that arises from deep within the earth. This pool is also fed by the stars within the earth, and its water contains the stellar energies that formed this world. Drink deeply from it.

- Draw the Altar and lay it down on the table to the right and next to the Stag and Pool card. As the stellar energies descend from the heavens and rise from the earth, they meet in you at your center, the altar of your being, where you are attuned to the wholeness. In you, the stars and earth, sun and moon meet and are made one in the flame of your sacredness. You are the place of synthesis where star and sun, moon and earth become one and become you.

- Draw the Edge and lay it down on the table to the right and next to the Altar card. You fly into the world, aloft on the wings of your wholeness. Though the world seems hard with materiality, your vision can see the stars shining under the surface. You are your star-self, revealing the stars within the world.

Here is what this layout looks like

Exercise 9: Attuning to the Sidhe

In presenting this exercise, Mariel said:

> One of the reasons we seek to work with you and have
> established the cards as a portal is because we feel when we
> attune to each other, our star-energy and star-nature induces
> a resonant response within your etheric body, drawing forth its
> stellar attunement. In other words, one way to attune to the stars
> within yourself is to attune to the stars within us.

Lay out the Stone Circle as shown on the back of the Manual and
imagine yourself entering the Howe at the center of the circle. In that
place, simply sit and welcome the presence of the Sidhe. If you wish to
draw a Dancer card to reflect or anchor this presence, feel free to do so.
You are there to jointly celebrate and attune to the stars within: the stars
within the earth, the stars within you, the stars within the Sidhe, the stars
within the cosmos.

Stay in the Howe in your imagination and contemplation as long as
you wish or as long as it feels comfortable to do so. When you feel ready,
or you feel tired or restless, thank the Sidhe for their presence. Turn over
the Dancer card and set it outside the circle, symbolic of their departure.
See yourself stepping out of the Howe and out of the circle, giving thanks
to the Stones and thanks to the Sidhe.

Gather up the cards and put them away.

You can do this exercise whenever you feel a need to realign and re-
attune to the Sidhe. However, remember, at some point, you don't need
the cards to do this, for you are a living Stone Circle, and the Howe is
within you, waiting for you to use it and to celebrate your wholeness at
the altar that it contains.

If you don't have a *Card Deck of the Sidhe*, you can still do this
exercise perfectly well. Just imagine yourself stepping into a circle of
great standing stones under a night sky. In the middle of this circle is a
hollow hill, the Howe. As you walk towards it with the stones around
you, the stars blaze in the sky above you, and as you enter the Howe,
you discover it is filled with stars and starlight as well, the stars within
the earth, the stars and starlight within you. You can then follow the

exercise as written.

Here is the image of the Howe from the card deck:

CONCLUSION
Final Thoughts

It has been a delight for me to work with the Sidhe these past few years. Their presence brings a joy and a lightness into my world that is special. Yet, it's also true that I've been a hesitant partner. I did not seek out this contact, but now that it is here and a part of my life, I've been doing my best to honor it.

Part of my challenge has been to understand just how to work with the Sidhe. I have over sixty years of experience working with subtle beings of one kind or another, and I know pretty well how to engage with them. I know what collaboration and partnership with a non-physical, spiritual being is like and what it can accomplish. I don't have anywhere near that same experience with the Sidhe. In many ways, they remain a mystery to me. What I'm keenly aware of is how much I don't know. But I'm learning, and I've appreciated their patience with me as I do.

There are three questions I always ask when dealing with the subtle worlds. The first two are: Does this contact help me to be a better person? Does this contact empower me to be a blessing for my world?

It may well be that a particular subtle being has nothing specific to offer in either of these cases, but neither does it take away anything. It may have overall a neutral effect, perhaps because it doesn't understand human life well enough or it's just too different from us to know how to contribute. But if any being diminishes my ability to be a functioning, integrated and balanced person or makes me less effective in being of service to my world, then that's a deal-breaker.

The third question is what can I do to assist the being with whom I'm in contact, i.e. how may I be a good partner?

In the case of Mariel and the Sidhe companions who accompany her, the answer to the first two questions has been a resounding yes. The answer to the third question is, I'm still figuring this out. Obviously, I've helped out by being a point of contact through which they could bring a card deck into the world and give voice to their thoughts. But this seems like just a start to me. What else is possible? What can any of us do to allow the Sidhe to be a practical presence in our lives and in our world?

We humans face serious issues in our world. So much about our civilization is broken and creating suffering, and we have been extending our brokenness out into the world as well with increasingly serious and devastating consequences. The Sidhe have much to offer us through their understanding of connectedness, wholeness, and the power of life. But are we ready to take lessons from beings whom most people can't see or hear and regard as the stuff of fantasy?

I know Mariel understands the problem, which is why she says not to focus on them but to take whatever inspiration they can provide to focus on our own capacities to understand and create wholeness. She says, "Find the Sidhe within you," and this is good advice. But it's still not easy to do.

One thing I have discovered about Mariel is how practical and "down-to-earth" she is. She wants to know what works, and usually what works best is what is specific.

The Sidhe have asked us to invite them into our lives to help and to ask for their assistance. There is no guarantee that they can help with what we want, but if we are specific in our request, it gives them something more concrete to work with, as well as making us more present and visible to them.

So, for instance, if I say that I would like the Sidhe to help me with world peace, there's not a lot to go on there other than good intention. How should they help? And what does world peace really mean to me other than as an abstraction? How do I work for world peace anyway? What specifically am I asking for?

If, on the other hand, I need help in making peace with my next-door-neighbor or with a co-worker at the office or at the store where I work, then this is more specific and plays to their strengths as beings of connection and harmony. It creates a very specific context that makes my energy more visible to them.

Similarly, if I ask the Sidhe to help bring healing and wholeness to nature, this is too abstract a request, and too unfocused a task. But if I ask their help in bringing fertility and beauty to a vacant lot in a city where I'd like to grow a small garden, this is specific and well within their capabilities as I understand it.

Of course, as I say, there is no guarantee that they can do what we ask or help with a particular situation. And some things we ask for may better be served by a subtle colleague operating from one of the dimensions of spirit. But as a rule of thumb, the more practical we can be in what we seek to do and in knowing how they might help, the better able the Sidhe are to engage with us.

Over the past three years since the publication of the *Card Deck of the Sidhe*—and especially through the class and the *Views from the Borderland* Subscriber's Forum—I've come to know many people who have formed partnerships with the Sidhe in their lives, receiving help in all manner of ways, from gardening to doing psychotherapy to helping out with manifestation in their businesses. I frankly do not know all the areas in which the Sidhe can help, nor do I know the limits upon their capacities to do so. This is what we discover by experimenting, and many people are experimenting. They are having practical, amazing results in so doing. Someday it would be wonderful to have a book that simply shares all these stories. They leave no doubt that the Sidhe can be very real and helpful partners.

However, we have to be careful not to think of the Sidhe simply as a new form of "servant" there to aid us in whatever way we may need. The helping is a side product of their deeper desire to bring wholeness back into Gaia's life, which, among other things, can help to correct the many environmental imbalances now occurring due to human activity. If we really want to partner with them, then the best way to do so is to seek ways ourselves that we can create the wholeness and healing that we and the planet need.

Finding in ourselves the human equivalent of the joy, the wonderment, the attunement to life, the skill in connectedness, and the creation of wholeness that mark the Sidhe is really what this work is about. This is what Mariel and her association seeks to foster. Whether we call it "finding the Sidhe Within" or "finding our deep and sacred humanity," it's what the world needs. It's what we need to do.

I hope this book provides help in this direction. I know this is Mariel's intent, and it's certainly mine as well. The information it contains probably raises as many questions as it answers, and it's not any kind of a final statement. Hopefully, it will inspire you to seek further. John Matthews, R.J. Stewart, Orion Foxwood, and Søren Hauge all have books that can provide more information. Undoubtedly, there are other resources out there as well.

But in pursuing the Sidhe, keep this in mind: the road to the Sidhe is through the starlit depths of our own humanity as a child of the Earth and a partner to Gaia. It is in finding and appreciating who we are that we can discover who we and the Sidhe are together.

Will there be other messages from Mariel? Well, if the past is any indication, I would say yes. As she herself has indicated, this is a long-term project. For me, it's been a series of peaks with valleys of preparation inbetween. The first peak was the card deck, the second was the Guardian Mantle exercise, and the third was the class. In between, there were ongoing contacts and a continuation of the energy links. Are there other peaks coming? Well, it's hard to say as I feel in a valley right now, but it wouldn't surprise me. If you'd like to keep in touch about this, you can do so through the Lorian mailing list. And the first place that new messages from Mariel or her associates may appear is in my esoteric journal, *Views from the Borderland*, which is available through Lorian.

I want to close this book with one of Jeremy Berg's beautiful paintings for the *Card Deck of the Sidhe*. In this picture, we see two roses, one white, one red, intertwined, while nearby sits a grail, a symbol of wholeness. In legends, the Sidhe are often represented by a white rose while humanity is a red one. Thus this picture is one of reconciliation and blending in a spirit of wholeness.

These are the same two roses found on the cover of this book. Reconciliation and partnership, the collaborative engagement of our two peoples is the theme that runs through all these conversations. It's the theme of the card deck. It's the theme of Mariel's work and that of her association. May it be our theme, as well.

**May the two roses bloom and intertwine in your life,
For your blessing and the blessing of the world.**

About the Author

David Spangler, lives in the Northwest, is married and has four children. He has been a spiritual teacher since 1964. From 1970-1973, he was a co-director of the Findhorn Foundation Community in Northern Scotland. In 1974 he co-founded the Lorian Association, a non-profit spiritual educational organization, and continues to work with it today. David is also a Fellow of the Lindisfarne Association, a gathering of scientists, mathematicians, artists, spiritual and religious teachers, ecologists, and political scientists, all interested in promoting a new culture based on holistic and Gaian values. For further information on his work, writings and classes, please visit www.lorian.org.

About the Artist

Jeremy Berg, MCS is owner of the Lorian Press and Starseed Publications and past Director of the Lorian Association. He was trained as an architectural designer and holds a patent for a panelized arch structural system. His work in energy efficiency and earth sheltered construction have appeared on the cover of Popular Science and other Magazines. He is a workshop presenter, holds a certificate in Spiritual Direction, has taught at both the secondary and post secondary level and been a college administrator.

About the Publisher

Lorian Press is a private, for profit business which publishes works approved by the Lorian Association. Current titles by David Spangler and others can be found on the Lorian website www.lorian.org.

The Lorian Association is a not-for-profit educational organization. Its work is to help people bring the joy, healing, and blessing of their personal spirituality into their everyday lives. This spirituality unfolds out of their unique lives and relationships to Spirit, by whatever name or in whatever form that Spirit is recognized. For more information, go to www.lorian.org.

Lightning Source UK Ltd.
Milton Keynes UK
UKOW06f1156160216

268471UK00014B/45/P